# The Sacramental Life

Simon Jones is Chaplain and Fellow of Merton College, Oxford, and also teaches liturgy in the Faculty of Theology in the University of Oxford and at St Stephen's House, Oxford. He wrote the introduction to the sixtieth anniversary edition of Gregory Dix's *The Shape of the Liturgy*, published by Continuum, and is also co-author of *Celebrating the Eucharist*, published by SPCK. He is an oblate of Elmore Abbey, the Anglican Benedictine community in Newbury to which Dix's community moved in 1987, and where the Dix archives are now held.

Other titles in the *Canterbury Studies in Spiritual Theology*

CANTERBURY STUDIES IN SPIRITUAL THEOLOGY

# The Sacramental Life

*Gregory Dix and His Writings*

*Edited by*

Simon Jones

CANTERBURY
PRESS
Norwich

© in this compilation Simon Jones 2007

First published in 2007 by the Canterbury Press Norwich
(a publishing imprint of Hymns Ancient & Modern Limited,
a registered charity)
13–17 Long Lane, London EC1A 9PN

www.scm-canterburypress.co.uk

British Library Cataloguing in Publication data

A catalogue record for this book is available
from the British Library

ISBN 978-1-85311-717-6

Typeset by Regent Typesetting, London
Printed and bound in Great Britain by
William Clowes Ltd, Beccles, Suffolk

# Contents

# Preface

I am very grateful to all those who have encouraged and assisted with the publication of this volume. In particular, thanks are due to the Archbishop of Canterbury, Dr Rowan Williams, for suggesting the idea of a Gregory Dix reader, and for contributing the Foreword; to Christine Smith, of SCM-Canterbury Press, for her enthusiasm for the project; to Continuum, publishers of *The Shape of the Liturgy*, and to all of Dix's previous publishers for granting copyright permission; to Judith Kirby, Fellows' secretary at Merton College, for her assistance with typing some of the texts; to Fr Benedict Green CR, for giving permission for two of Dix's letters to his father to be included in this volume; and, not least, to the current members of Dom Gregory's community, the monks of Elmore Abbey, for their generosity in allowing me to transport the Dix archive to Merton in order to work on it.

The texts included in this volume have been taken from a number of published and unpublished sources. Each passage is prefaced by a brief introduction, and several footnotes have been added to provide context or identify individuals, but otherwise Dix is allowed to speak for himself. His writings pre-date a concern for inclusive language, but in order to remain faithful to the original, the generic use of 'man' and 'mankind' has been retained. A number of passages have been abridged, and this is indicated by bold ellipses.

As a Christian, priest and religious, Dom Gregory Dix lived and was nourished by a sacramental life. It is my hope that fresh exposure to the richness of his writings will encourage others to imitate his example of sacramental living.

*Simon Jones*
*Merton College, Oxford*
*April 2007*

# Foreword

## by the Archbishop of Canterbury

The Church of England is not always good at giving full recognition to its few real original geniuses. Austin Farrer, despite his high reputation during his lifetime, has long tended to be the preserve of a few enthusiasts, and only fairly recently has he begun to receive anything like his proper share of appreciation more widely. Gregory Dix has had an even harder fate: he is known – to those who've heard of him at all – as the author of a long book on the liturgy, whose conclusions are no longer generally accepted, and perhaps as the author of one specially resonant paragraph which often appears in devotional guides to the Eucharist ('Was ever another command so obeyed? . . .').

But those who have read and re-read *The Shape of the Liturgy* as something more than an historical study will want to claim a lot more. Yes, the book contains several astonishing passages in addition to the one just referred to, passages that ought to stand among the finest pieces of religious writing in English in the twentieth century. But more importantly – and more importantly than the details of the rightness or wrongness of his historical conclusions – *The Shape* offers a shape for the whole of Christian thinking. Its central image is the single movement of the Son to the Father, in eternity and in time: the outpouring of the Son to the Father in the Trinity, to borrow Karl Barth's language, 'the journey of the Son of God' to the cross and the resurrection, with the great pivotal sign of the Lord's Supper summing up and holding the meaning of that journey and opening out on to the perspective of eternity again, and the Son's return to heaven with the redeemed creation in his hands, a return which comes to its conclusion at the end of time – a 'second coming' which in fact is one and the same with the whole of that eternal journey. Within this divine movement, God's journey into God, we find our life and our hope, the judgement of all we are and have been, the gift that renews us and transforms every relation, social and personal, so that we can speak, in Dix's wonderful phrase, of *homo eucharisticus*, the renewed human species that is defined in and through the Eucharist.

This big book is a lot more than an essay on liturgical history. Almost every page abounds in wit and insight, and the great rhetorical passages still have power to stop the reader in his or her tracks. The whole book evokes as few others do a sense of what it is simply to inhabit the Christian universe, a world centred upon the Word made flesh. Dom Gregory never wrote anything else quite like it; but he did write a good deal apart from *The Shape*, and it is the same vision that pervades all these slighter works. Because so many of these are to be found only on the shelves of retreat house libraries – those Valley-of-the-Kings deposits of inextricably mingled treasure and rubbish – it is a real gift to have their finest elements extracted and presented here in accessible form. Here we see most clearly how Dom Gregory brought the immensities of his theological vision to bear on the bread and butter of learning to live Christianly and to pray intelligently.

He was an inveterate and indiscreet ecclesiastical politician, of course, and some of the passages here presented give a strong flavour of the mischief that he could gleefully make for a rather self-important establishment. But that is rather the point: he made mischief because he had so little time for church arguments that showed no theological integrity and that relied upon pragmatic solutions or appeals to an establishmentarian common sense. What he writes about ordained ministry is anything but conciliatory, nothing like the blandnesses of some sorts of ecumenical consensus; but it is always just as distant from a repetition of self-serving orthodoxies. His analyses of the origins and growth of the episcopate may, like his liturgical theories, be open to all sorts of challenge, and scholarship has moved on; but these pages are full of ideas that can still change the whole landscape of the conventional reader's world.

This book is in a very robust sense a joy to read: Dix always wrote with enormous elegance and energy and often exceptional beauty, as well as wit. But more profoundly, the vision he spells out in practically every page of his writing is one that should generate joy and gratitude to God for the richness of his revelation and action in our history. Simon Jones has done an excellent job in quarrying Dom Gregory's work, published and unpublished, and has done a great deal to confirm him as a true theological giant. I hope these pages will send many to the books themselves; more than that, though, I hope they will do what he would of course have wanted – to send people to the altar, to the place where the journey of the Son of God, the coming of the Messiah to the Father, is opened to us day by day.

+ Rowan Cantuar
From Lambeth Palace
*Visitation of the Blessed Virgin Mary to Elizabeth, 31 May 2007*

# Abbreviations

| | |
|---|---|
| CP | *The Christian Passover* |
| DA | *A Detection of Aumbries* |
| DCNT | *Dixit Cranmer Et Non Timuit* |
| GWM | *God's Way with Man* |
| HO | *Holy Order* |
| ICPL | *The Idea of 'the Church' in the Primitive Liturgies* |
| ILG | *The Image and Likeness of God* |
| JEC | *'Jurisdiction in the Early Church'* |
| JG | *Jew and Greek: A Study in the Primitive Church* |
| MEC | *The Ministry in the Early Church* |
| PC | *The Parish Communion* |
| PWG | *The Power and Wisdom of God* |
| QAO | *The Question of Anglican Orders* |
| RC | *'The Revealing Church'* |
| SL | *The Shape of the Liturgy* |
| TL | *The Liturgy* |

# Introduction

On 10 September 1962, Eric Mascall wrote the following letter to the Abbot of Nashdom, Dom Augustine Morris:

Christ Church,
Oxford

10 September 1962

My dear Father Abbot

Last night the Regius Professor of Divinity, Dr Henry Chadwick, was saying how important he thought it was that Dom Gregory's papers and a selection of his letters (especially the latter) should be published before a new generation comes into being which has never known him. So I write to pass on the point to you!

I remember that a long time ago there was some such suggestion and that Michael Ramsey was then anxious to write an introductory memoir, but nothing seemed to come of this. Has the idea been abandoned or is someone in charge of it still?

Since Dom Gregory's untimely death in 1952, a deep respect for Dix's writings and for their author have led to several attempts to make his work more widely known. Michael Ramsey was the first to be asked to undertake this project, not long after Dix's death. Henry Chadwick took up the baton in the 1960s, and correspondence between an American publisher, Morehouse-Barlow, and Dom Patrick Dalton, another monk of Dix's community, suggests that a Lent book providing a daily reading from Dix's writings was also destined for publication, but never completed. Several posthumous volumes of sermons, retreat addresses, lectures and articles did, however, appear in the 25 years after Dix's death, and excerpts from these are included in this volume. More recently, Simon Bailey made use of the archival material at Elmore Abbey to provide a detailed assessment of Dix's life in his 1995 biography, *A Tactful God*.

Those who, 45 years after Mascall's 'generation', know the name Dom Gregory Dix are most likely to have encountered him through his magisterial work *The Shape of the Liturgy*, which has remained in print since it was first published in 1945. However, as Ramsey, Chadwick and others have recognized, the 'fat green book', as Dix affectionately referred to it, though the best-known and most significant of his writings, represents only one relatively small part of his total literary output. The present volume is the latest attempt to make the varied writings of Nashdom's most celebrated monk known to a new generation by rediscovering some forgotten treasures as well as revealing for the first time some that have hitherto remained hidden. These have been divided into four sections, which explore the way in which Dix has shaped the Church's liturgy, its spirituality, its religious life and its ministry.

George Eglington Alston Dix was born in London on 4 October 1901. Educated first in Eastbourne and then at Westminster School, Dix went up to Merton College, Oxford, in 1920 to read history and left three years later with a second class degree. After a short period of ordination training at Wells Theological College, he returned to Oxford in October 1924 to be ordained as tutor and lecturer in modern history at Keble College. Dix's stay at Keble was short-lived, and after just two years he moved to the Anglican Benedictine Abbey at Pershore, shortly before the community itself moved to Nashdom Abbey, in Burnham, Buckinghamshire. Built by Lutyens for a Russian prince, Nashdom is a Russian word which means, literally, 'our home', and the rapidly growing community of monks soon made it such, transforming the baroque ballroom into a chapel for its daily round of worship.

Dix was clothed as a novice in 1926 and took the name Gregory. The following year he was sent to the community's house in the Gold Coast (Ghana), St Gregory's Priory. There the monks were responsible for running St Augustine's Training College, as well as the local parish, St Cyprian's. Although Dix was well equipped to contribute both to the teaching and pastoral work required of the community, his African experience came to an abrupt end in 1929 when he developed appendicitis and was eventually invalided home.

Based again at Nashdom, Dix found time for writing and research. He contributed a number of articles to the community's journal *Laudate* before, more significantly, producing a critical edition of *The Apostolic Tradition of St Hippolytus*, published in 1937. This was intended to be a two-volume work, but Dix's preoccupation with

*The Shape* meant that volume 2, the commentary, was never written. Very few contemporary scholars would share Dix's theories about the authorship, dating and significance of this document as a witness to early liturgical practice;[1] yet, thanks in no small part to Dix's edition, the *Apostolic Tradition's* influence over subsequent liturgical revision has been immense, and its witness to what was believed to be a primitive Eucharistic prayer continues to provide the model for a number of contemporary liturgical texts, not least in the most recent Church of England revision, *Common Worship* (2000).[2]

Of even greater influence, however, has been Dix's monumental work *The Shape of the Liturgy*, first published in January 1945. The fruit of 14 years of research and 14 months of writing, *The Shape* heralded a new era in the study of liturgy, and still has a well-deserved place on bibliographies as recommended reading for those beginning liturgical study. One of the reasons why the influence of this work has endured for so many years is the attractive simplicity of its central thesis. Distancing himself from those who believed that there was a common verbal core to primitive Eucharistic rites, Dix maintains:

> By careful analysis there is to be found underlying most of these varying rites and most of the older ones a single normal standard *structure* of the rite as a whole. It is this standard structure which I call the 'Shape' of the Liturgy. (*SL* xi)

For Dix, the original 'shape' is the 'seven-action scheme' of Jesus at the Last Supper, in which Jesus took bread, gave thanks over it, broke it and distributed it, saying certain words; and after the meal took the cup, gave thanks over it and distributed it, saying certain words. In a relatively short period of time, Dix believes that this 'seven-action scheme' was transformed into a liturgical fourfold shape which has 'constituted the absolutely invariable nucleus of every eucharistic rite known to us throughout antiquity from the Euphrates to Gaul' (*SL* 48). This fourfold shape embodies the taking of the bread and the cup, thanksgiving over the elements, the breaking of the bread, and the distribution of the elements.

Whilst marvelling at the influence which this thesis has exerted over liturgical scholarship and revision, it's interesting to note that, whereas Dix and contemporary liturgical scholars have now, by and large, parted company,[3] 60 years on the imprint of Dix's fourfold shape can still be clearly traced in the Eucharistic rites of many Anglican Provinces as well as other Christian denominations.[4] This suggests that, whereas the fourfold shape may no longer be recognized as the 'invariable nucleus' of primitive rites, it is likely to remain the model for contemporary revisions for a number of years to come.

Any assessment of Dix's considerable literary output during the 1930s and 1940s must take account of the role which the liturgy at Nashdom played in forming Dix's own spiritual life. With its Latin mass and offices from the Roman Missal and Breviary, this Anglican Benedictine community made a very clear statement about its ecclesiology and self-consciously asserted its Catholic identity within the Church of England. This identity Dix embraced wholeheartedly, but it also led him to question where the ecclesial boundaries of his own vocation to the priesthood and religious life should lie. His journey towards life oblation was marked by frequent uncertainty as to whether he should convert to Roman Catholicism. This, coupled with his experience of ill health in Ghana, led him to leave the novitiate in 1929 and transfer to being an 'intern oblate', until he re-entered the novitiate in 1936, and on 11 October 1940 made his life profession at West Malling Abbey.

Whatever doubts Dix may have had about his relationship with Anglicanism, the evidence of many of his later writings, and not least his popular *The Question of Anglican Orders: Letters to a Layman* (1944), suggests that he 'passionately' believed in the Church of England and, as far as its Catholic identity was concerned, had no hesitation in affirming that, 'Unless we are "Catholics" inasmuch as and *because* we are "Anglicans", then we are not being "Catholics"' (QAO 9).

Having convinced himself of the Catholic identity of the Church of England, Dix became an enthusiastic evangelist of this position, seeing it as his task to convince others to recognize it, and to speak out against attempts to deny or undermine it. Long before his election as a Proctor in Convocation for the Diocese of Oxford in 1945, Dix made no secret of his opposition to the proposal for a united Church of South India, in which Anglican, Methodist, Presbyterian and Congregationalist churches would be joined together in one ecclesial body. For Dix, the fatal ecclesiological flaw in such a plan was its willingness to jettison a Catholic understanding of episcopacy for the sake of union with non-episcopal churches, and to recognize the validity of the orders of those who had not been episcopally ordained. Although proposed for church communities far from the Provinces of Canterbury and York, Dix feared that the Church of England would look to imitate such a plan as a model for Church union at home, with the result that the prospect of reunion with Rome would become an even more distant dream.⁵ Dix's strength of feeling on this matter cannot be underestimated. In the last of his letters to Harry in *QAO* he writes:

> I think some of us would never be altogether happy again if what these good and sincere men hope for in South India and elsewhere were to come to pass. We should have a choice of wilderness in which to serve the Lord – and that would be about all. (*QAO* 88)

In expressing such a view Dix had a number of powerful allies, not least his friend and diocesan bishop Kenneth Kirk. Kirk's book of essays, *The Apostolic Ministry* (1946), was written against the background of the South Indian controversy, and Dix's contribution, though perhaps not his most convincing piece of scholarship, was nevertheless one of the most significant to have appeared in that volume.

A tireless and prominent political campaigner as well as a popular writer, Dix was in constant demand as a preacher, retreat conductor and lecturer. His diaries reveal a gruelling schedule of frequent engagements which sometimes took him away from Nashdom for weeks at a time. Such was Dix's reputation that, as well as finding himself at home in the pulpits of some the great Anglo-Catholic shrines, where his romantic and expansive prose would undoubtedly have wooed sympathetic congregations, he also received invitations to preach in more unlikely locations, such as St Paul's Cathedral, and Great St Mary's, Cambridge, where he gave a University Sermon in 1946.

Among some of Dix's most profound works are his spiritual writings, particularly his retreat addresses. In these we see a side to Dix which is very unlike the boisterous, provocative Church politician. Included in this volume are some excerpts from his *Retreat on the Holy Rule* as well as an address on prayer from a Christmas retreat given to the Sisters of the Church in 1938. Here we see commonsense, practical advice articulated out of a deep conviction that all prayer, be it private or public, is a corporate activity. Making use of his favourite Pauline image, he describes prayer as being offered by the community of the Church, the Body of Christ, the prayer of the members being caught up into the self-offering of the Son to the Father. 'There are no isolated Christians', Dix affirms. 'The head needs the members'.

As a lecturer Dix travelled widely. In 1950 he gave a series of lectures on the early Church in Uppsala, Sweden, which were post-

humously edited by Harry Carpenter and published under the title
*Jew and Greek* in 1953. Either side of this visit to Sweden, he made
two trips to the United States, first in 1947 and then again in 1950–
1. Nashdom had set up a daughter-house in the United States, St
Gregory's Priory in Three Rivers, Michigan. In its early days the
house experienced a number of problems, and Dix was sent to the
United States to help sort them out. On his first visit he recognized
that the buildings at St Gregory's were too small for the needs of
the community, particularly if it was going to grow. An adaptation
of the existing buildings and the building of a new chapel were proposed, but this would require a significant amount of fundraising
and the community was already facing financial difficulty. When Dix
arrived in 1947, both *The Shape* and his edition of *Apostolic Tradition* had just been published in the States. Recognizing, to his great
surprise, that he was in popular demand as a lecturer, preacher and
after-dinner speaker, Dix seized the opportunity as a means of fundraising. On both visits he subjected himself to a punishing schedule,
as one of his letters to Frederick Green (24 September 1951) indi-
cates. However, by the end of his second visit he had received almost
$30,000 in fees from speaking engagements and had raised a further
$100,000 from donations. This remarkable achievement allowed the
building work at St Gregory's to be completed, but at a much greater
cost to Dix's own health. The same letter to Frederick Green reveals
that he had been diagnosed with an intestinal cancer in November
1950. Since the building work had already begun and the American
Priory faced bankruptcy if the money wasn't raised, Dix postponed
surgery for eight months so that the lecture tour could continue and
the project be completed. He remained in the States long enough to
see the dedication of the new chapel on 3 May 1951, flew home the
following day, and went straight into hospital. Although the initial
operation had appeared to be successful, he did not have time to
recover fully before secondaries developed, leading to a final period
of illness. Gregory Dix died at Grovefield House, near Nashdom, on
12 May 1952, aged 50, and was buried four days later at the monks'
cemetery at the Abbey.

In the obituary which appeared in *The Times* a week after his
death, John Rawlinson, Bishop of Derby, wrote:

By the death of Gregory Dix the Church of England has lost one of
her most gifted and distinguished sons. A historian and scholar of
no mean order, he had also a highly original cast of mind (reflected

in his massive and learned *Shape of the Liturgy*) – qualities which, together with an impish sense of humour and a streak of sheer naughtiness, made his company a constant delight to those who were fortunate enough to be his friends. He was a superb raconteur and an extremely lovable man.

The selection of Dix's writings which follows has been chosen to reflect these diverse qualities of mind and personality. Although there are inevitably a number of gaps, the combination of scholarly writings, retreat addresses, sermons and letters is intended to highlight areas of interest in Dix's life which have had a lasting influence on the life of the Church, or at least have an enduring relevance for a number of contemporary issues.

It's tempting to speculate what additional impact Dix might have had on the life of the Church had he lived another 20 or 30 years. In the debate concerning the ordination of women, for example, one might reasonably assume that he would have favoured the 'ecumenical argument', opposing any departure from apostolic order by permitting women to enter the threefold ministry. However, in a tantalizingly incomplete article entitled 'The Ministry of Women', Dix begins his introduction by stating that 'I have reason to believe that neither the advocates nor the opponents of female clergy will be wholly pleased with its contents'. We can only wonder what its conclusion would have been.

What we can affirm with a much greater degree of certainty is that underlying and uniting the great majority of Dix's writings is the notion of sacrifice. For Dix, a sacramental life is a life lived sacrificially. So, for example, in the Eucharist,

> It is the whole Christ, the Incarnate Redeemer, who is present . . . acting as Incarnate, *by Sacrifice*, for our redemption. Sacrifice comes first; the Consecration and the Presence must be viewed primarily as effecting the *reality of the Sacrifice*, the Sacrifice by Christ of himself, and in him of all his members. (*TL*112)

For an Anglo-Papalist such as Dix, such an emphasis on sacrifice is not surprising. But it is by no means confined to his Eucharistic theology. At the conclusion of his meditation on the seventh word from the cross, his final Good Friday address preached in the Church of the Resurrection, New York, exhausted from his travels around America and painfully aware of the cancer within him, Dix describes death as the ultimate sacrifice of love:

Death is a solemn and serious thing, even for those who are full of faith and are prepared to die. It should be a ritual act, an act of worship . . . Supremely, it is an act of sacrifice to God . . . It is the total gift of oneself to the beloved that is the ideal of love, of human love in this life, and that is only a faint image of the total self-giving which is the Love of God. There is only one way: to let go of self, to give oneself to God out of love, the love that responds to His, manifested and demonstrated to the end on Calvary. (*GWM* 73–5)

Sacrifice also beats at the heart of Dix's understanding of vocation, not least vocation to the religious life. In a letter written to Marcus Stephens, he urges his friend who is wrestling with where his vocation might lie to: 'Give, give, give – that is what you have to do – to God, to your brethren, to the Church, to the world – never to yourself'. But this advice is not given to others without first being applied to himself. For Dix's understanding of sacrifice was most eloquently expressed in his own life, with its sacrificial commitment to his community at Nashdom and in the United States; to the Anglo-Catholic movement and the religious life; to the work of reunion with Rome and the promotion of the Catholic identity of the Church of England; and, not least, to his family and friends. His many letters reveal the genuine love and affection of a delightfully candid and, at times, unguarded, correspondent, whose life, sacramentally nourished and sacrificially lived, remains an outward and visible sign of the vocation of all God's people.

## Notes

1. See, for example, P. F. Bradshaw, M. E. Johnson, L. E. Phillips, *The Apostolic Tradition: A Commentary* (Fortress Press, 2002).

2. For example, Prayer B in Order 1 (modern language). Dix himself set the Hippolytan prayer to the Sarum tone, and on his two visits to America and at several Catholic Congresses in England used the *Apostolic Tradition* as the basis for dramatic reconstructions of the 'Primitive Liturgy'.

3. See, for example, the introduction to Paul Bradshaw, *Eucharistic Origins* (SPCK, 2004).

4. For a detailed assessment of its influence over both liturgical scholarship and revision, see the introduction to the new edition of *SL*, published by Continuum in 2005.

5. Dix was involved in the discussions between Anglicans and members of the Free Churches which resulted in the report *Church Relations in England* (1950).

# Gregory Dix –
# A Biographical Outline

| | |
|---|---|
| 1901 | Born in Woolwich, London on 4 October (named George Eglington Alston) |
| 1915–20 | Westminster School (King's Scholarship) |
| 1920–3 | Merton College, Oxford (Exhibitioner) |
| 1923 | BA in Modern History (Second Class) |
| 1924 | Ordinand at Wells Theological College; ordained deacon on 5 October |
| 1924–6 | Lecturer in Modern History, Keble College, Oxford |
| 1925 | Ordained priest on 4 October |
| 1926 | Entered Novitiate at Pershore Abbey; moved with community to Nashdom Abbey at Burnham, Buckinghamshire |
| 1927 | St Gregory's Priory and St Augustine's Training College, Gold Coast (Ghana) |
| 1929 | Transferred from Noviciate to Intern Oblate |
| 1936 | Re-entered Novitiate at Nashdom Abbey on 4 October |
| 1937 | Temporary Vows |
| 1939–41 | Interim priest at St Michael and All Angels, Beaconsfield |
| 1940 | Solemn Profession (at West Malling Abbey) on 11 October |
| 1945 | Publication of *The Shape of the Liturgy* |
| 1945–52 | Proctor in Convocation (Diocese of Oxford) |
| 1947 | St Gregory's Priory, Three Rivers, Michigan, USA (February–September) |

1948      MA (Oxon)

1948–52   Prior of Nashdom Abbey

1949      BD, DD (Oxon)

1950–1    St Gregory's Priory, USA

1952      Died at Grovefield House (near Nashdom) on 12 May;
          buried at Nashdom on 16 May

*Part One*

# Shaping the Liturgy

# The Shape of the Liturgy

*Gregory Dix is remembered first and foremost as a liturgical scholar, whose greatest achievement was undoubtedly* The Shape of the Liturgy, *published in 1945. Although contemporary scholars are less certain than they once were about many of Dix's hypotheses, it is difficult to underestimate the impact this book has had over liturgical scholarship and revision in the last 60 years.*

## The Eucharist and Society

*This passage, from the end of the introduction to the first edition of* SL, *dated Corpus Christi 1943, describes the Eucharist as a model for Christian living which is in opposition to the materialistic spirit of the age.*

In this period of the disintegration and attempted reconstruction of thought about our secular society, the individual's relation to society and his need for and securing of material things are the haunting problems of the age. There is a Christian pattern of a solution which is expressed for us and by us at the eucharist. There the individual is perfectly integrated in society, for there the individual Christian only exists as a Christian individual inasmuch as he is fully exercising his own function in the Christian society. There his need of and utter dependence upon material things even for 'the good life' in this world is not denied or even ascetically repressed, but emphasised and met. Yet his needs are met from the resources of the whole society, not by his own self-regarding provision. But there the resources of the society are nothing else but the total substance freely offered by each of its members for all. There, too, is displayed a true hierarchy of functions within a society organically adapted to a single end, together with a complete equality of recompense.

But the eucharist is not a mere symbolic mystery representing the right order of earthly life, though it is that incidentally and as a consequence. It is the representative act of a fully *redeemed* human life. This perfected society is not an end in itself, but is consciously and

wholly directed to the only end which can give meaning and dignity to human life – the eternal God and the loving and conscious
obedience of man in time to His known will. There the eternal and
absolute value of each individual is affirmed by setting him in the
most direct of all earthly relations with the eternal and absolute
Being of God; though it is thus affirmed and established only through
his membership of the perfect society. There the only means to that
end is proclaimed and accepted and employed – man's redemption
through the personal sacrifice of Jesus Christ at a particular time
and place in human history, communicated to us at other times and
places through the church which is the 'fulfilment' of Him. That is
the eucharist. Over against the dissatisfied 'Acquisitive Man' and his
no less avid successor the dehumanised 'Mass-Man' of our economic-
ally focussed societies insecurely organised for time, Christianity sets
the type of 'Eucharistic Man' – man giving thanks with the product
of his labours upon the gifts of God, and daily rejoicing with his
fellows in the worshipping society which is grounded in eternity. This
is man to whom it was promised on the night before Calvary that he
should henceforth eat and drink at the table of God and be a king.
That is not only a more joyful and more humane ideal. It is the divine
and only authentic conception of the meaning of all human life, and
its realization is in the eucharist.

(*SL* xxxviii–xxxix)

## The Performance of the Liturgy

*This passage comes from the beginning of the second chapter of* SL,
*entitled 'The Performance of the Liturgy: Saying and Doing'. Here
Dix argues that the Eucharist is primarily an action in which the
whole Church has a part to play. Although, in the Roman Catholic
Church, encouragement of the laity to active participation in the
Eucharist can be traced back to Prosper Guéranger (1805–75) and
Pius X (1835–1914), Dix's emphasis on the Eucharist as a corporate
action of priest and people anticipates the call to full, conscious and
active participation of the reforms of the Second Vatican Council.*

If such an abstraction as 'the general conception entertained by the
typical Anglican priest or layman of what the eucharist fundamentally
is' can be analysed, it will be found, I believe, that he thinks of it primarily as something which is *said*, to which is attached an action, the

act of communion. He regards this, of course, as an essential con-
stituent part of the whole, but it is nevertheless something attached
to the 'saying', and rather as a consequence than as a climax. The
conception before the fourth century and in the New Testament is
almost the reverse of this. It regards the rite as primarily something
*done*, of which what is said is only one incidental part, though of
course an essential one.

   In pointing such a contrast there is always a danger of making
it sharper than the realities warrant. But in this case I am confi-
dent that the contrast is really there. The modern conception is not
characteristic of any one 'school of thought' in modern Anglicanism, or indeed confined to Anglicanism at all, but is true of modern
Western devotion as a whole, catholic and protestant alike. We all
find it easy and natural to use such phrases as, of the clergy, '*saying* mass', and of the laity, '*hearing* mass'; or in other circles, 'Will
you *say* the Eight?' or '*attending* the early Service'. The ancients on
the contrary habitually spoke of '*doing* the eucharist' (*eucharistein
facere*), '*performing* the mysteries' (*mysteria telein*), '*making* the
synaxis' (*synaxin agein, collectam facere*) and '*doing* the oblation'
(*oblationem facere, prosphoran poiein*). And there is the further contrast, that while our language implies a certain difference between
the functions of the clergy and the laity, as between active and passive
('*taking* the service' and '*attending* the service'; '*saying*' and '*hearing*' mass), the ancients used all their active language about 'doing'
the liturgy quite indifferently of laity and clergy alike. The irreplaceable function of the celebrant, his 'special liturgy', was to 'make' the
prayer; just as the irreplaceable function of the deacon or the people
was to *do* something else which the celebrant did not do. There was
difference of function but no distinction in kind between the activities of the various orders in the worship of the whole church.

(SL 12)

## The 'Four-Action' Shape of the Eucharist

*The corporate Eucharistic action which Dix describes in Chapter 2
is further defined at the beginning of Chapter 4 as a fourfold shape,
derived from the 'seven-action scheme' of the Last Supper. This
central thesis of* SL *drives Dix's own agenda for liturgical reform.*

The last supper of our Lord with His disciples is the source of the liturgical eucharist, but not the model for its performance. The New Testament accounts of that supper as they stand in the received text present us with what may be called a 'seven-action scheme' of the rite then inaugurated. Our Lord (1) took bread; (2) 'gave thanks' over it; (3) broke it; (4) distributed it, saying certain words. Later He (5) took a cup; (6) 'gave thanks' over that; (7) handed it to His disciples, saying certain words. We are so accustomed to the liturgical shape of the eucharist as we know it that we do not instantly appreciate the fact that it is not based in practice on this 'seven-action scheme' but on a somewhat drastic modification of it. With absolute unanimity the liturgical tradition reproduces these seven actions as four: (1) The offertory; bread and wine are 'taken' and placed on the table together. (2) The prayer; the president gives thanks to God over bread and wine together. (3) The fraction; the bread is broken. (4) The communion; the bread and wine are distributed together.

In that form and in that order these four actions constituted the absolutely invariable nucleus of every eucharistic rite known to us throughout antiquity from the Euphrates to Gaul.

(SL 48)

## The Pre-Nicene Eucharist celebrated in Brondesbury

*At the beginning of Chapter 6, to describe the celebration of a pre-Nicene Eucharist in Rome, Dix uses a more familiar setting to great effect.*

It is very easy for us to romanticise the life and worship of the primitive Christians. What was conventional in the social setting of their day has for us the picturesqueness of the strange and remote; what was straightforward directness in their worship has for us the majesty of antiquity. It is a useful thing occasionally to transpose it all into the conventions of our own day and look at the result.

Suppose you were a grocer in Brondesbury, a tradesman in a small way of business, as so many of the early Roman Christians were. Week by week at half-past four or five o'clock on Sunday morning (an ordinary working day in pagan Rome) before most people were stirring, you would set out through the silent streets, with something in your pocket looking very like what we should call a bun or a scone. At the end of your walk you would slip in through the mews at the back of one of the big houses near Hyde Park, owned by a wealthy

Christian woman. There in her big drawing-room, looking just like it did every day, you would find the 'church' assembled – socially a very mixed gathering indeed. A man would look at you keenly as you went in, the deacon 'observing those who come in' [*Didascalia* 2.57] but he knows you and smiles and says something. Inside you mostly know one another well, you exchange greetings and nod and smile; (people who are jointly risking at the least penal servitude for life by what they are doing generally make certain that they know their associates). At the other end of the drawing-room sitting in the best arm-chair is an elderly man, a gentleman by his clothes but nothing out of the ordinary – the bishop of London. On either side of him is standing another man, perhaps talking quietly to him. On chairs in a semicircle facing down the room, looking very obviously like what they are – a committee – sit the presbyters. In front of them is a small drawing-room table.

The eucharist is about to begin. The bishop stands and greets the church. At once there is silence and order, and the church replies. Then each man turns and grasps his neighbour strongly and warmly by both hands. (I am trying to represent the ancient by a modern convention. The kiss was anciently a much commoner salutation than it is with us in England, but it implied more affection than does merely 'shaking hands' with us.) The two men by the bishop spread a white table-cloth on the table, and then stand in front of it, one holding a silver salver and the other a two-handled silver loving-cup. One by one you all file up and put your little scones on the salver and pour a little wine into the loving-cup. Then some of the scones are piled together before the bishop on the cloth, and he adds another for himself, while water is poured into the wine in the cup and it is set before him. In silence he and the presbyters stand with their hands outstretched over the offerings, and then follow the dialogue and the chanted prayer lasting perhaps five minutes or rather less. You all answer 'Amen' and there follows a pause as the bishop breaks one of the scones and eats a piece. He stands a moment in prayer and then takes three sips from the cup, while the two men beside him break the other scones into pieces. To each of those around him he gives a small piece and three sips from the cup. Then with the broken bread piled on the salver he comes forward and stands before the table with one of the deacons in a lounge suit standing beside him with the cup. One by one you file up again to receive into your hands 'The Bread of Heaven in Christ Jesus', and pass on to take three sips from the cup held by the deacon, 'In God the Father Almighty and in the Lord

Jesus Christ and in the Holy Spirit in the holy church', to which you answer 'Amen'; then you all file back again to where you were standing before. There is a moment's pause when all have finished, and then most of you go up to the bishop again with a little silver box like a snuff-box into which he places some fragments of the Bread. You stow it in an inside pocket, reflecting perhaps that Tarcisius was lynched six months ago for being caught with one of these little boxes upon him. There is another pause while the vessels are all cleansed, and then someone says loudly, 'That's all. Good morning, everybody.' And in twos and threes you slip out again through the back door or the area door and go home – twenty minutes after you came in. That is all there is to it, externally. It would be absolutely meaningless to an outsider, and quite unimpressive.

(*SL* 142–3)

## Liturgical Fear and Prejudice

*In the midst of a description of the context of persecution in which the pre-Nicene Church celebrated the Eucharist, Dix uses a humorous reminiscence of his Methodist grandmother to draw attention to the nonsense of liturgical prejudices, simultaneously revealing his own Anglo-Papalist tendencies.*

When we regard what actually took place in the early eucharistic rite, the fear and hatred it inspired over so long a time seem ridiculous. Yet it is an uncanny fact that there is still scarcely any subject on which the imagination of those outside the faith is more apt to surrender to the unrestrained nonsense of panic than that of what happens at the catholic eucharist. As a trivial instance, I remember that my own grandmother, a devout Wesleyan, believed to her dying day that at the Roman Catholic mass the priest let a crab loose upon the altar, which it was his mysterious duty to prevent from crawling sideways into the view of the congregation. (Hence the gestures of the celebrant.) How she became possessed of this notion, or what she supposed eventually happened to the crustacean I never discovered. But she affirmed with the utmost sincerity that she had once with her own eyes actually watched this horrible rite in progress; and there could be no doubt of the deplorable effect that solitary visit to a Roman Catholic church had had on her estimate of Roman Catholics in general, though she was the soul of charity in all things else. To all suggestions that the mass might be intended as some sort of holy communion service she replied only with the wise and gentle pity of the fully-informed for the ignorant.

(SL 145–6)


## The Eucharist and the Body of Christ

*This passage, from Chapter 9, reveals the importance of sacrifice within Dix's Eucharistic ecclesiology. Just as Christ offered himself to the Father as a 'pledged Victim' at the Last Supper, so at the offertory, the first action of the fourfold shape, the Church offers herself to the Father, that she may become what she will receive – the Body of Christ.*

The unity (rather than 'union') of the church's eucharist with the sacrifice of Christ by Himself is one consequence of the general pre-Nicene insistence on the unity of Christ with the church, of the Head with the members, in one indivisible organism. We have noted Irenaeus' picturesque phrase that in her oblation 'that poor widow of the church casts in all her *life* into the treasury of God'. [*Against Heresies* 4.18.2] The church corporately, through the individual offertory by each member for himself or herself personally, offers itself to God at the offertory under the forms of bread and wine, as Christ offered Himself, a pledged Victim, to the Father at the last supper. The Body of Christ, the church, offers itself to *become* the sacrificed Body of Christ, the sacrament, in order that thereby the church itself may become within time what in eternal reality it is before God – the 'fullness' or 'fulfilment' of Christ; and each of the redeemed may 'become' what he has been made by baptism and confirmation, a living member of Christ's Body . . . As Augustine was never tired of repeating to his African parishioners in his sermons, 'So the Lord willed to impart His Body, and His Blood which He shed for the remission of sin. If you have received well, you *are* that which you have received'. [*Sermon* 227] 'Your mystery is laid on the table of the Lord, your mystery you receive. To that which you are you answer "Amen", and in answering you assent. For you hear the words (of administration) "the body of Christ" and you answer "Amen". Be a member of the Body of Christ that the Amen may be true.' [*Sermon* 272]

Because the oblation of Himself to the Father by Christ is ever accepted, that of the church His Body is certain of being blessed, ratified and accepted too. The offertory passes into consecration and communion with the same inevitability that the last supper passed into Calvary and the 'coming again' to His own. But the unity of Christ and the church is not something achieved (though it is intensified) in communion; it underlies the whole action from start to finish.

It is the firm grasp of the whole early church upon this twofold meaning and twofold truth of the phrase 'Body of Christ' and their combination in the eucharist which accounts for those remarkable passages, commonest in St Augustine but found also in other writers, which speak almost as though it was the church which was offered and consecrated in the eucharist rather than the sacrament . . .

There is a deep truth in this way of regarding the eucharist, which is slowly being recovered to-day by the clergy, though it is to be feared that the English lay communicant has as a rule little hold upon it. As the *anamnesis* of the passion, the eucharist is perpetually *creative* of the church, which is the fruit of that passion.

(SL 247–8)

## The Fourth Century as a Turning Point in Human History

*This passage, from the end of Chapter 11, on 'The Sanctification of Time', is a wonderful example of the rich, romantic and poetic language which characterizes the prose of* The Shape.

So the last Christian generation of the old Roman world looked wistfully into the future knowing the end had come, and turned to God. In all its unhappiness and its carnality that world had always loved beauty; and now at the end there was given it a glimpse of the eternal Beauty. And it cried out in breathless wonder with Augustine, 'Too late have I loved Thee, Beauty so ancient and so new!' [*Confessions* 10.27]

There is a sort of pause in events round the turn of the century while that whole ancient world – still so magnificent – waits for the stroke of God, and trusts Him though it knows He will slay. It is like some windless afternoon of misty sunshine on the crimson and bronze of late October, when time for an hour seems to stand still and the whole earth dreams, fulfilled and weary, content that winter is at hand. The whole hard structure of the *civitas terrena*, the earthly city that had once thought itself eternal, was now ready to dissolve into a different future. Gibbon was right. The foundation of the empire was loosened by the waters of baptism, for the empire's real foundation was the terrible pagan dream of human power. Its brief Christian dream of the City of God which alone is eternal was broken by the roaring crash of the sack of Rome by the Goths in A.D. 410. The world went hurrying into the darkness of seven long barbarian centuries, but pregnant now with all the mediaeval and modern future. It was the achievement of the church in the single century that had passed since Diocletian that, though all else changed in human life, it was certain to be a Christian world, that centred all its life upon the eucharist.

(*SL* 395–6)

## The Command Never So Obeyed

*This, the most well-known and best-loved of all* The Shape's *purple passages, is the first of two to be quoted from its final chapter. Here again, Dix emphasizes the ubiquity of the unbroken action of the fourfold shape, the manifestation of the 'sheer, stupendous quantity of the love of God', whose divine origins lie in the Last Supper.*

At the heart of it all is the eucharistic action, a thing of an absolute simplicity – the taking, blessing, breaking and giving of bread and the taking, blessing and giving of a cup of wine and water, as these were first done with their new meaning by a young Jew before and after supper with His friends on the night before He died. Soon it was simplified still further, by leaving out the supper and combining the double grouping before and after it into a single rite. So the four-action Shape of the Liturgy was found by the end of the first century. He had told His friends to do this henceforward with the new meaning 'for the *anamnesis*' of Him, and they have done it always since.

Was ever another command so obeyed? For century after century, spreading slowly to every continent and country and among every race of earth, this action has been done, in every conceivable human circumstance, for every conceivable human need from infancy and before it to extreme old age and after it, from the pinnacles of earthly greatness to the refuge of fugitives in the caves and dens of the earth. Men have found no better thing than this to do for kings at their crowning and for criminals going to the scaffold; for armies in triumph or for a bride and bridegroom in a little country church; for the proclamation of a dogma or for a good crop of wheat; for the wisdom of the Parliament of a mighty nation or for a sick old woman afraid to die; for a schoolboy sitting an examination or for Columbus setting out to discover America; for the famine of whole provinces or for the soul of a dead lover; in thankfulness because my father did not die of pneumonia; for a village headman much tempted to return to fetich because the yams had failed; because the Turk was at the gates of Vienna; for the repentance of Margaret; for the settlement of a strike; for a son for a barren woman; for Captain so-and-so, wounded and prisoner of war; while the lions roared in the nearby amphitheatre; on the beach at Dunkirk; while the hiss of scythes in the thick June grass came faintly through the windows of the church; tremulously, by an old monk on the fiftieth anniversary of his vows; furtively, by an exiled bishop who had hewn timber all day in a prison camp in Murmansk; gorgeously, for the canonisation of S. Joan of Arc – one could fill many pages with the reasons why men have done this, and not tell a hundredth part of them. And best of all, week by week and month by month, on a hundred thousand successive Sundays, faithfully, unfailingly, across all the parishes of Christendom, the pastors have done this just to *make* the *plebs sancta Dei* – the holy common people of God.

To those who know a little of Christian history probably the most moving of all reflections it brings is not the thought of the great events and the well-remembered saints, but of those innumerable millions of entirely obscure faithful men and women, every one with his or her own individual hopes and fears and joys and sorrows and loves – and sins and temptations and prayers – once every whit as vivid and alive as mine are now. They have left no slightest trace in this world, not even a name, but have passed to God utterly forgotten by men. Yet each of them once believed and prayed as I believe and pray, and found it hard and grew slack and sinned and repented and fell again. Each of them worshipped at the eucharist, and found their thoughts wandering and tried again, and felt heavy and unresponsive and yet knew – just as really and pathetically as I do these things. There is a little ill-spelled ill-carved rustic epitaph of the fourth century from Asia Minor: – 'Here sleeps the blessed Chione, who has found Jerusalem for she prayed much'. Not another word is known of Chione, some peasant woman who lived in that vanished world of Christian Anatolia. But how lovely if all that should survive after sixteen centuries were that one had prayed much, so that the neighbours who saw all one's life were sure one must have found Jerusalem! What did the Sunday eucharist in her village church every week for a lifetime mean to the blessed Chione – and to the millions like her then, and every year since? The sheer stupendous *quantity* of the love of God which this ever repeated action has drawn from the obscure Christian multitudes through the centuries is in itself an overwhelming thought. (All of that going with one to the altar every morning!)

(SL 743–5)

## The Eucharist as a Theory of Human Living

*This passage brings the 752-page* Shape *to its conclusion. As a corporate activity, the Eucharist is described as 'the whole life of the Church', saving humanity from self-sufficiency and enabling it to act out its freedom of dependency upon God.*

The eucharist is the whole life of the church and of the Christian expressed, fulfilled, done, in an action; for as Goethe (I think) says somewhere, 'the highest cannot be spoken, it can only be acted'. The more we can learn to think of our own worship at the eucharist not in terms only of assistance at a pleading or recollection of a redemption two thousand years ago, nor yet in terms only of 'my communion' (however true these partial understandings may be), but in terms of the 'pan-human' fulfilment of the Messianic sacrifice, the nearer we shall be to entering into the mind of the apostolic church about the eucharist and the further from most of our present controversies.

'There is one human race in which the mysteries of God are fulfilled'. It has been said that the problem of our generation will be the *motive* of civilisation. But in fact that is the problem in one form or another of all generations, the theory of human living. It has only been made more acute for us by the progressive apostasy of the liberal tradition in Europe for the last three centuries. The dream of the self-sufficiency of human power has haunted the hearts of all men since it was first whispered that by slipping from under the trammels of the law of God, 'Ye shall be Gods', choosing your own good and evil. (Gen. 3.5) . . .

In the eucharist we Christians concentrate our motive and act out our theory of human living. Mankind are not to be 'as Gods', a competing horde of dying rivals to the Living God. We are His creatures, fallen and redeemed, His dear recovered sons, who by His free love are 'made partakers of the Divine nature'. (2 Pet. 1.4) But our obedience and our salvation are not of ourselves, even while we

are mysteriously free to disobey and damn ourselves. We are dependent on Him even for our own dependence. We are accepted sons in
the Son, by the real sacrifice and acceptance of His Body and Blood,
Who 'though He were a Son, yet learned He obedience by the things
which He suffered; and being made perfect, He became the author
of eternal salvation unto all them that obey Him; called of God an
High-priest after the order of Melchisedech'. (Heb. 5.8f.)

(*SL* 751–2)

## Worship as a Witness to Christian History

*Jew and Greek is a posthumous collection of lectures which Dix
gave, first, at Uppsala, Sweden, in February 1950, and later in
America. In this passage, at the end of a survey of two generations of
Christian history (described as the predominantly Jewish-Christian
'Apostolic' generation and the predominantly Gentile-Christian
'sub-Apostolic' generation), Dix discusses worship as a witness to
Christian history.*

As one tries to understand that bewildering history *as* history, there
are two cautions to be remembered. One is that religions pray.
Academics, historians and theologians forget that. They have to
follow the course of events and ideas. But for the average person,
prayers and rites and conduct, these are 'religion', in any faith.
Behind all the individual actors and events and documents of the
first Christian century we can never forget the multitude of anony-
mous Christian men and women scattered in groups thickly or thinly
all over the Mediterranean world, believing 'the Gospel', living by
'the Gospel', suffering for 'the Gospel', handing on 'the Gospel', worshipping by 'the Gospel', which they had received by a multitude of
different channels. It means that no single individual, not Peter or
Paul or Mark or John, was ever in a position entirely to *control* the
Gospel by his own understanding of it. It is in '*the life of the Church*'
(or 'the Spirit' or 'the Paraclete') that the real springs of the history
lie. And to this our most direct clue lies in the *worship* by which the
Church lived. Anything which bears on that will help to explain the
history.

   Secondly, one has to remember that history happens through men
and women, not through abstractions. We talk of 'Hellenisation'
and 'Jewish' conceptions. We must – but these are 'averages'. Who

is to say, in so complex a history, what was 'Greek' and what was 'Jewish-Christian' in the minds of men like Timothy or Titus with their Greek background and their adult circumcision and their long companying with Jewish Christians like St Paul, besides their incessant contacts with Greeks and half-Greeks and 'God-fearers' and Hellenistic Jews and Christian Pharisees and Jewish Nationalists and all the rest? In the generation after A.D. 65 there must have been an infinity of gradations even among the leaders – men like Timothy, Titus, Luke, Mark, Linus and the rest – the extent of their individual responses to 'Hellenic' and 'Judaic' ideas. What they all lived for and by was 'the Gospel' . . .

What we have to remember is that there were not two forces at work in the mind of the sub-Apostolic Church, Hellenism and Judaism, but three. There was also 'the Gospel'. And there was a power in 'the Gospel' to be itself, to master both the Jew and the Greek, to reject and to select and to choose, which is the more impressive the more it is studied. On the most naturalistic view possible of the history it is still true that Jesus did not cease to operate in it after A.D. 30. On the contrary, Jesus, what He was and did in Galilee and Judaea, continued to dominate and control what happened 'in the Messiah' through all the transition. To ignore that renders the whole story unintelligible.

(*JG* 109–11)

## The Christian Passover

*This passage is taken from an article first published in Nashdom's own journal,* Laudate, *in 1935 and republished in the same year as a pamphlet by the Church Literature Association. The article is too long to be included in its entirety. However, the introduction and conclusion provide a good example of Dix's combative prose style, with which he argues for the abolition of the Anglican practice of 'ante-communion' on Good Friday with an unashamedly Anglo-Papalist interpretation of the practice of the early Church.*

The following notes have a twofold purpose. The first is the hope that they may be of some little help to the piety of those who assist at the Liturgy of the Pre-Sanctified on Good Friday . . . The second, but no less virtuous purpose – that of sticking one or two pins into those loyal theorists who invariably defend the limitations of the official

Anglican mentality with the ambiguous excuse that its manifestations are "primitive". There is an increasing and laudable deference
among us to the universal tradition that the Sacrament should not be
consecrated on this day. But there has also sprung up a less praiseworthy theory of the liturgiologists (some eminent names might
be quoted) that the "primitive" observance of Good Friday was by
an unliturgical *synaxis* or Mass of the Catechumens, a service of
lessons, psalmody and intercessions answering very roughly to our
"ante-communion", and that the Eucharistic worship at the climax
of the rites of the Pre-Sanctified is a later accretion. I venture to assert
that this is demonstrably the exact reverse of the historical facts, and
would have been examined and rejected by Anglican scholars long
ago but for the tendency to canonise the only use possible in the
current Anglican rite . . .

I have no wish to suggest either that we should cease to observe
Good Friday or that Communions should be multiplied on that day,
though it is worth remembering that it is only in the last three centuries that the Communion of the Pre-Sanctified has been restricted
to the celebrant. But in these days of more frequent Communion
the very abstinence from it on Good Friday has its own emphasis.
Devotional habits and conventions change, though I fancy that devotional instincts change very little. Good Friday observance, indeed,
offers a singular example of this. To judge by the amount of current
suggestion and experiment for its improvement the provision which
Cranmer made for public worship on this day is not being found very
satisfactory, but the innovators are clearly finding themselves in a
cleft stick. On the one hand the reviving Sacramental sense of Anglicanism in general instinctively feels that liturgical worship which has
no Eucharistic centre of any kind is somehow a little frustrated; on
the other our regained feeling for tradition and liturgy is leading to
an increasing deference to the unbroken rule of antiquity that there
shall be no *consecration* on that day. East and West have solved the
dilemma with the reserved sacrament, but the official Anglican way
out, the "ante-communion" alone, has everywhere proved itself too
jejune and pointless to become a popular devotion. It is generally
recited to a comparative handful, while the bulk of the laity do the
best they can with the unliturgical "Three Hours". This is exactly
what happened when the Roman Church introduced the equivalent
of "ante-communion" as the central liturgical observance of Good
Friday in the fifth or sixth century. The *people* felt the need of a
more expressive worship on this day, and supplemented the Stational

"ante-communion" with the unliturgical "Veneration" in the parish churches. And the mind of the Church, East and West, deep rooted in the devotional instincts of the Christian people, clung to St Paul's dictum that in the "eating" and "drinking" (not the "breaking" and "blessing") of the bread and the cup lies *the* proclamation of the Lord's death. And in the end the devotion of the people forced the official liturgy to answer their needs. It may be that even *Ecclesia Anglicana* will one day learn not to trust exclusively to overworked human throats. Listening to sermons, however excellent, is not a substitute for *worship*, and the "Three Hours" offers the absolute minimum of opportunity for that thankful adoration by the redeemed which is presumably the purpose of the day. It may be that in the great lack of any effective opportunity for worship in most of our churches on this day lies one cause of the increasing secularisation of Good Friday.

The theory that the "ante-communion" only is primitive on Good Friday is a tendentious legend. Those who celebrate it are merely acting in strict accord with an innovation in the personal liturgy of the Popes in the Dark Ages. Nor is there any better foundation for the plea that it is in any historic sense "Anglican". There is nothing whatever in the Prayer Book to suggest that it contemplates anything but a celebration of the entire rite, complete with the thunders of Sinai and the *Gloria in excelsis*. If three communicants give in their names at least some time the day before, the parson is presumably bound to celebrate. And it is a certain fact that most representative Anglicans, *e.g.*, Queen Elizabeth, Lancelot Andrewes, Dr. Johnson and the Prince Consort, habitually made their communions on Good Friday at celebrations conducted in this fashion. It was, indeed, the true "primitive" instinct of devotion, but if reservation is to be excluded it is impossible to be "primitive" in practice on this day.

Meanwhile we may envy – though we are told we must not imitate – the Roman Church, which on Good Friday has added to her own archaic rites, enshrining the piety of the Apostolic age itself, things new and old drawn from the treasuries of younger Churches and later times, as though she would gather all Christendom with her about the Cross. It is a touch of that genius for understanding the depths of the human soul which in every age has moved multitudes of common men instinctively to call the Roman Church their "Mother", for all her imperious tones and jealous ways. That is an august and tender title which it is much to be wished the common man would more often bestow elsewhere. One can only speculate as to how quickly he will be induced to do so by encountering the rich imagination and the ardent tender joy of redemption which insist upon the Decalogue as the opening devotion in the liturgy of Good Friday.

(CP 2–3, 16–17)

## The Liturgical Movement

*This passage concludes Dix's essay 'The Idea of "the Church" in the Primitive Liturgies' which he contributed to the influential volume,* The Parish Communion, *edited by his friend Gabriel Hebert SSM, and published by SPCK in 1937. It was subsequently republished by the same publisher as a separate pamphlet. Here Dix links the aims of the Liturgical Movement with a sacrificial understanding of the Eucharist.*

The "Liturgical Movement", now rapidly growing in strength in the French and German Churches, has at least begun among the exiled Russians, and in the Greek *Zoe* movement, and in various ways among ourselves. It is no merely ecclesiological or archaeological fad. It seeks to return behind the medieval "clerical" distortion of the eucharist to the truer and deeper conception of the Church of the Martyrs, only because it has first recovered a more authentic notion of what is involved in the doctrine that the Church is the mystical Body of Christ, that the sovereign Spirit of the Risen Life of Jesus is the very breath of her life. It will be found that just in those quarters where the Liturgical Movement has obtained the strongest hold, there that new longing for the unity of all Christians, that new Catholic zeal for scientifically truthful historical studies, that new Catholic demand for social reforms, that new Catholic energy of Apostolate among those that have not the faith, both at home and abroad, have also found their most remarkable developments. This is not surprising. Where the Church is true to her calling as the Body of Christ, she must needs offer herself and all her members in sacrifice to God in union with the sacrifice of her Head. Like Him she can only find *thus* the consummation and fulfilment of her life in the world. And in Him this sacrifice of herself is perpetually accepted, perpetually fruitful "for the life of the world". But its price is a continual "dying to the world" that she may live, for she is "not of the world" as her Lord is "not of the world", and it must needs be that the world should hate that which is not its own, the "redemption" it perpetually needs.

These things are all in the eucharist, rightly understood. St Augustine said them long ago in words that have never been surpassed:

"The Congregation and Society of the Saints is offered in an universal sacrifice to God by the High Priest, who offered even Himself in the form of a servant for us in His passion, that we might be the Body of so great a Head. This form of a servant He offered, in this He was offered; for this He is mediator and priest and sacrifice. And so the Apostle exhorted us that we should present our bodies a living sacrifice, holy, pleasing to God, our reasonable service, and that we be not conformed to this world but reformed in the newness of our mind, to prove what is the will of God, that which is good and well-pleasing and complete; which whole sacrifice we ourselves are . . . This is the sacrifice of Christians: 'The many one Body in Christ'. Which also the Church celebrates in the sacrament of the altar, familiar to the faithful, wherein she is shown that in this that she offers, she herself is offered to God." [*City of God* 9.6]

(PC 142–3)

## Reverence for the Reserved Sacrament

*Provision for reservation of the sacrament was one of the reasons why the 1927/8 revision of the Book of Common Prayer was rejected by Parliament. As an Anglo-Catholic, Dix was a strong advocate of reservation. In his study* A Detection of Aumbries, *published by Dacre Press in 1942, he gives an account of the history of Eucharistic reservation and argues for different methods of reservation being favoured by the Church in different geographical locations. Although subsequent generations of scholars have, by and large, dismissed Dix's theory, in this passage he moves from the historical to the theological and examines the Church's understanding of Eucharistic presence, with particular reference to primitive practice and the Church of England. Although Dix claims that he doesn't want this study to contribute to 'current controversies', he does not try very hard to conceal his own opinions when he claims that the general trend of the 'whole of Christian tradition' is that the presence of Christ is related 'very closely to the eucharistic elements'.*

As regards the geographical prevalence of particular methods of reservation in the later middle ages, we may say that broadly speaking the aumbry is the prevailing Italian and Spanish way, the sacrament-house is German and Dutch, the tabernacle is French and Rhenish, and the hanging pyx is English and Norman or North French. This does not mean that one cannot find occasional exceptions in most countries to the prevailing local fashion. There is, for instance, the lovely bronze 'goblet' receptacle for the sacrament made by Becchietta for the altar of Siena Cathedral in the 13th century, which has features derived from the hanging pyx, sacrament-house and tabernacle in combination, and represents perhaps a further subdivision; we have already noted the isolated appearance of a hanging pyx at Farfa in Italy and of a tabernacle in England. French practice varied more than that of other countries even as late as the 18th century. Broadly speaking, this geographical division of methods holds good from, say, the later 13th century to the 16th.

But these are the mere external facts. If we would really understand the history of developments in these things we must, I believe, take account of an influence of which we have hitherto said little, but which was really the governing factor in the history of changes in methods of reservation; I mean, the varying notions of what constitutes 'reverence' for the consecrated species in different ages and places.

We are treading here on delicate ground. Anglicans hold different convictions of a passionate sincerity on doctrinal questions which are very apt to be imported into the purely historical questions at issue, all of which convictions one would wish to treat with seriousness and respect, whatever one's own chosen stand. These things lie very near to the heart of the religion of all Christian men, in a region where instinct rightly plays as large a part as reason. I would wish to be understood as trying to write history and to reflect upon it, rather than as making a contribution to current controversies or as advocating the adoption of any particular practices among ourselves.

I think that anyone who should examine carefully the history of English Episcopal legislation in the 13th century which has been cursorily sketched above, and its apparently total failure to achieve its object, would be bound to reach the conclusion that fundamentally it represents a conflict between the precision of official Latin theological theory and a profound popular instinct of Englishmen, and indeed of the Northern peoples generally, as to what constitutes 'reverence'.

Behind all the 13th-century English Episcopal injunctions one can discern, simply from the language employed, a single impulse, viz. the decree of 1215, defining the dogma of transubstantiation, and by consequence ordering the custody of the reserved sacrament in an aumbry. And behind the continuous and nationwide disobedience to the plain commands of the English bishops there lay not so much mere nationalism and conservatism – after all, we picked up other foreign ways in worship both in the 13th and the 16th centuries without all this difficulty – but something which goes much deeper into our national character and temperament. The motives of the bishops are obvious enough. They acted partly out of a respect for the law as such, but chiefly from a determination not to allow practice to go beyond the dictates of strict theological theory as then officially understood at Rome. It is remarkable how many of the 13th-century Episcopal regulations about aumbries are set in a little doctrinal homily on the official teaching about the sacrament of the altar, which is generally as remarkable for what it carefully does not say as for what it does. On the other hand, behind the resistance of the clergy there is something which comes out very rarely indeed in the official documents, though we have already twice encountered expressions of it from Lyndwood and from the Devonshire rebels: 'The English custom is praiseworthy in this, that the sacrament is more readily brought before our eyes that we may *worship* it'; 'We will have the sacrament to hang over the high altar and there to be *worshipped* as it was wont to be.'

Bishop Westcott, as so often, pierced to the heart of the matter when he wrote: 'I shrink with my whole nature from speaking of such a mystery, but it seems to me to be vital to guard against the thought of the Presence of the Lord in or under the forms of bread and wine. From this the greatest practical errors *follow.*' [*Life and Letters of B. F. Westcott,* vol. 2, p. 351]

It may be said that such language is very closely in line with much that was taught by our Reformers, especially by Archbishop Cranmer, though it seems hardly reconcilable with our present Anglican formularies taken as a whole, especially with the language of the Prayer Book Catechism. By its changes from the second Prayer Book of Edward VI and especially by its restoration of the words, 'The Body . . .' and 'The Blood of our Lord Jesus Christ, etc.', in the form of administration, the Elizabethan Prayer Book did, apparently intentionally, reopen doors which Cranmer had intended to shut fast, and the Church of England has never since closed them. The general trend of the interpretation of the eucharist by the whole of Christian tradition, East and West alike, and especially of pre-Nicene tradition, is in the direction of relating the Presence very closely to the eucharistic elements. And though the New Testament Scriptures have too often been canvassed by all parties for it to be worth while at this stage to appeal to them afresh in support of particular views, at the same time since the 'Words of Institution' and St Paul's language about 'discerning the Lord's Body' are to be found there, it cannot be denied that the essential relation of the Presence to the elements is at least a wholly legitimate doctrine.

Westcott's views are not my own, but it must be recognised that he goes to the root of the matter in making all else hinge on the vital question whether 'the Presence of the Lord' is or is not 'in or under the forms of bread and wine'. If it is not, then amongst other consequences reservation in itself is entirely meaningless and probably pernicious. The very fact that reservation in some sort is to be traced back to the early 2$^{nd}$ century is in itself a sufficient commentary on early eucharistic doctrine. If, on the other hand, the Presence is 'in or under the forms of bread and wine', then the view which may be summed up under the phrase: 'The eucharist is the Body and Blood of Christ, and as such to be adored whenever and wherever it is found', is not difficult to justify.

For my own part, I do not doubt that the first half of this phrase is the authentic, original and true Christian doctrine. The second would appear to be a logical and indeed inevitable corollary. Yet it must in reality be a rather less simple one to see than it appears to many today. There is, for instance, the curious fact that it does not seem to have suggested itself quite in that form to Pope Innocent III, either before or after his definition of transubstantiation. It is quite true that as one studies the 2$^{nd}$-century Christian writers and comes upon phrases like that in the earliest description of Christian worship in Justin Martyr: 'The (Bread and Wine) which has been made eucharist *is* – (*einai*, no word could be stronger) – the Flesh and Blood of that Jesus who was made flesh', [*Apology*, 1.66] one comes to recognise that there was a directness about the 'realism' of sub-apostolic teaching on the eucharist which I find for myself comes less easily to one brought up on our more guarded Anglican formulae. Nor is it, as has too often been said, only of the sacrament 'in action', as it were, of the sacrament being received in holy communion, that such language was used. The reserved Bread is for Hippolytus 'the body of Christ' (*soma Christou*) without qualification, even when it is being nibbled by a mouse. It is 'the holy body' for Optatus, even when it is being profanely cast to dogs. It is for Novatian 'the holy Body' even when it is being carried around by the careless Christian 'amidst the vile bodies of harlots'. No one attentively considering the language of pre-Nicene writers could suppose that, whatever their precise belief

may have been, they had even thought of that 'receptionism' by which
some Anglicans since Hooker have sought to avoid both the complete
dissociation of the Presence from the elements on which Westcott
was (from his own standpoint) so clear-sightedly insistent, and also
those 'great practical errors' or consequences which he was so sure
followed from any other view.

(DA 42–6)

## Cranmer the Zwinglian

*Published originally in the* Church Quarterly Review *of 1948, Dix
wrote 'Dixit Cranmer Et Non Timuit' in response to G. B. Timms's
paper, 'Dixit Cranmer', which had appeared two years earlier, originally as a paper read before the annual meeting of the Alcuin Club
in May 1946. By arguing forcefully that 'Cranmer in his eucharistic doctrine was a devout and theologically-founded Zwinglian',
Dix was not only making an historical-doctrinal observation, but
also building a case for radical revision of the Book of Common
Prayer against those of the 'modern High Church party' who, like
Timms, preferred to believe that Cranmer was a sort of 'premature
Tractarian'.*

It is always with sympathy – though tinged sometimes with melan-
choly apprehensions – that one comes upon representatives of the
modern High Church party engaged in the first-hand study of our
English Reformers and the genesis of our English Prayer-book. To be
frank, a good deal of such study by such people will be needed if we
are to get rid of a mischievous legend which did much to stultify the
discussion of Prayer-book revision a generation ago – viz., that Archbishop Cranmer was a sort of premature Tractarian whose Books
of Common Prayer were intended to express – or at the very least
to include – anything like the doctrine so dear to the Tractarians of
an "objective Real Presence" in or under the consecrated bread and
wine of the Eucharist. It may be true, as Darwell Stone once wrote,
that there was "something providential in the notion of the Tractarians that they had support for their position in a post-Reformation
tradition, because without this belief they very likely would not have
had the heart to go on." [Letter to Lord Halifax, 27 January 1914]
But even in 1914 that wise scholar felt constrained to add, "We have
now to face the facts", which were other than the Tractarians had

imagined. Those facts were not faced then, and they have generally been concealed since, with results in Anglican life that we all know, even if we do not care to trace them to their causes. If they are not treated more seriously and more realistically before Prayer-book revision again becomes a practical question, then the result, so far as the eucharistic rite is concerned, is likely to be only a second botch which Churchmen at large will quietly but decisively decline to use. And I for one do not care to contemplate the practical consequences to the life of the English Church of another frustration of that kind.

These among other considerations weighed with me when I reluctantly decided to include in a book called *The Shape of the Liturgy* (1945) some conclusions on Archbishop Cranmer and his English Prayer-books. These were that Cranmer in his Eucharistic doctrine was a devout and theologically-founded Zwinglian, and that his Prayer-books were exactly framed to express his convictions. The publication of these ideas was received, as I regretfully foresaw that it would be, with distress by many of those devout souls whom one would least desire to trouble. Among High Churchmen (in the stiffer sense of the term) they were denounced as "tendentious", "irresponsible" and even "inexcusable". If I am any judge, this part of the book has caused uneasiness among the clergy, but by and large its conclusions have not been fully accepted, and the purpose of publishing them was not understood. Yet except for the cursory dissent of some reviewers, they received no historical criticism which could reasonably claim the notice of an explanation.

It was therefore with some interest that I learned that the Rev. G. B. Timms had come forward under the appropriate banner of the Alcuin Club with a reasoned criticism, in a paper which was subsequently printed in the *Church Quarterly Review*. To my great satisfaction, I found that Mr. Timms, starting with an ecclesiastical standpoint and purpose so different from my own, had reached conclusions on some of the essential questions identical with mine. It is true that at times he seems more anxious to emphasise our differences than to record agreements. But for my part I am happy to find how extensively we agree; and I am sure that, notwithstanding some imperfections, the circulation of his pamphlet cannot fail to do much good among the followers of the Alcuin Club, both in helping them to overcome their prejudices and positively in preparing them to recognise the truth about the Prayer-book. I propose, therefore, to take this opportunity of approaching these topics again. By using Mr. Timms's paper as a peg rather than a target, and supplementing his evidence and conclusions as occasion serves, I hope it may be possible to carry the historical question a step forward.

We agree – I use Mr. Timms's words so far as possible – that

(i)    "Not only does he (Cranmer) deny transubstantiation; he denied any real objective presence in the sacred elements *per se* at all."

(ii)    Cranmer "rigidly refuses, even where the context might lead us to expect it, to make (any) 'instrumental' identification of the elements with the body and blood . . . they are, however, a divine 'seal' or 'guarantee', promises of effectual signification 'that Christ does feed us with his body and blood' [*at the moment we receive them*: they are temporally but not ontologically identified] . . . But he (Cranmer) will not say that Christ feeds us *through* the elements". (Italics Mr. Timms's.)

(iii)    For Cranmer, the Eucharistic sacrifice consists exclusively "of praise and thanksgiving, together with an offering of ourselves" – as contrasted with any "pleading" of the Sacrifice of Christ, or any offering of his body and blood to the Father, or any sort of oblation of the elements, consecrated or unconsecrated, in any sense whatever.

(iv)    Cranmer's answer to the question "Is the spiritual gift which is received in holy communion essentially different from that which is received in spiritual communion?" – was "obviously" a decided negative.

It will be observed that except for the clauses about which I have made some demur in (ii), the whole statement is negative; and also that if there is not an actual contradiction between these clauses and (iv), at all events there is some difficulty in adjusting them, on any basis which involves an *objective* spiritual gift of any kind appropriated in, or by the reception of, the Sacrament (such as *e.g.* was taught in his later years by Calvin). Nevertheless Mr. Timms sets out to show that Cranmer was not (as I termed him) a Zwinglian, but what he calls a "dynamic-receptionist", and he couples him explicitly with Bucer and Calvin as teaching this doctrine.

Calvin, I suggest, is better left out of the picture altogether. That "instrumental" relation of the elements to the body and blood of Christ which Cranmer "refuses" was the very pivot of Calvin's fully-developed teaching, and the word *instrumentum* is a usual term with him. It is true, too, that Calvin in the forties of the sixteenth century was still feeling his way to the "Calvinist" eucharistic doctrine, which assumed completeness only with the third edition of the *Institutes* in

1559. At the critical period of the English Reformation it is doubtful how far Calvin ought to be described as a "Receptionist". Early in 1549, by the *Consensus Tigurinus*, he had reached an agreement with the Zwinglians, including their extreme left wing under Megander, in which he had gone very far indeed to meet their negative views. It is significant that he was never again willing to use the language which he used at this time. There is nothing in the evidence, however, to suggest that Cranmer himself or the Edwardian Reformers generally, then or earlier, paid any special attention to Calvin's views. The period of his influence on the English Reformers came later, after the accession of Elizabeth. In King Edward's time the English Protestants looked rather to Bullinger and Zürich. A typical instance of these variations is to be found in John Jewel. After serving as notary to Cranmer and Ridley in their Oxford disputations he fled abroad early in 1555. But at Frankfort he quarrelled with Knox and the Calvinistic party, and fled on to Zürich where Bullinger received him. It is not surprising to find him in the closest epistolary and doctrinal connection with Zürich[A] during the first three or four years of Elizabeth's reign. Later the connection cools, and he becomes one of the theological leaders of a reaction towards a Calvinist Receptionism.

Bucer, however, is a different matter. In 1548 he had failed (for the second time) to agree about the Eucharist with even the more moderate Zwinglians, and had left Zürich in something of a huff. Hooper, who was then living at Zürich, imbibing truth from the source, wrote after him a fussy letter intended to be consoling, and begged him not to take his dismissal too much to heart: "Away with those who would sow dissension between you and these men. I promise you, they very frequently make mention of you in friendly and honourable terms. And though they may dissent from your opinion in the matter of the eucharist, as I do myself, yet they do not make any breach in Christian love, much less regard you with hostility."[B] With his usual happy tact, Hooper goes on to treat poor Bucer as a Lutheran, offering to "prove easily to the satisfaction of every one" that he is all wrong, and ending with a commendation of the charity of the Zwinglians who were grieved at Luther's death, "not as if they had lost an adversary and detractor". But twenty years of intermittent colloquies and memoranda between Luther and Bucer had already failed to produce any effective agreement on the Eucharist, as clearly as they had failed to reconcile the Zwinglians with either of them. Bucer had in fact made an attempt to elaborate a mediating doctrine between Lutheranism and Zwinglianism somewhat along the lines finally worked out by Calvin; but then, as later, there could be no genuine reconciliation of two such contradictory positions, and both parties had ended by washing their hands of Bucer. Lutherans and Zwinglians alike expressed a malicious pleasure when he was compelled by Charles V to flee from Strassburg in 1549 and took refuge in England. His teaching, as found *e.g.* in his *Confessio de Eucharistia* (1550)[C] is much nearer to the Swiss than to the Lutheran view, but it can fairly be described as "Receptionist", and it was being propagated as such in England during the critical period of the Edwardian Reformation. He does repeatedly make something like that "instrumental" connection of the elements with the body and blood which Cranmer rejected and Calvin accepted, though he prefers to say that the "Presence" (he uses and defends the term) is *per usum* rather than *per symbola* or *per panem et vinum*, and he makes it depend solely on the subjective faith of the communicant. Though such teaching would by no means have satisfied Dr Pusey or St Justin Martyr, it closely resembles that of most modern Anglican "Evangelicals". Bucer teaches indeed a doctrine of the "Real Presence", though in the most attenuated form possible without lapsing into the "Real Absence" of Zwingli. Yet the difference between them is more than a question of labels, and Bucer himself – taught by his rebuffs at Zürich – was somewhat polemically conscious of that difference. The question "Was Cranmer a Zwinglian or a Bucerian?" is therefore important for our purpose, and I am grateful to Mr. Timms for raising it plainly, for I must confess that I neglected it in *The Shape of the Liturgy*. The very fact that the question now forces itself upon an High Churchman in that particular form is in itself an indication of coming changes in the outlook of that party. The legends are dissipating.

(*DCNT* 1–6)

## Notes

A. *Zürich Letters* (1st Series), ed. Robinson, Parker Soc., 1842, i–lxxvii, *passim*. See *e.g.* p. 21: "We have exhibited to the Queen all our last articles of religion and doctrine, and have not departed in the last degree from the confession of Zürich." (Jewel to Bullinger from London, 28 April 1559)

B. Hooper to Bucer, 19 June 1548. *Original Letters*, xxv, ed. Hastings Robinson, Parker Soc., 1846, p. 45.

C. *Scripta Anglicana*, Basle 1577, pp. 538ff. See esp. 33–36, 43–45, and 54. It is more satisfactorily expressed in his *Censura* (1551), but only in incidental statements (see esp. cap. ix pp. 473ff.).

## Moments of Consecration

*This is the final section of a paper on eucharistic consecration read at the Priests Convention in Tewkesbury in May 1938. The subject of the Convention was 'The Liturgy' and all the papers were subsequently published in the same year in a volume edited by the Bishop of Brechin, Kenneth Mackenzie. Dix notes that his published paper was slightly rewritten after the Convention to take account of points raised in discussion. To this gathering of Anglo-Catholic clergy, Dix argues that any exposition of a high doctrine of consecration and real presence has to be built upon the firm foundation of eucharistic sacrifice: 'Sacrifice comes first; the Consecration and the Presence must be viewed primarily as effecting the reality of the Sacrifice, the Sacrifice by Christ of himself, and in him of all his members.'*

I have spoken of the idea of a "moment of consecration" as a somewhat late development, and of our expression of that idea in the Elevation as altering the balance of Eucharistic doctrine and devotion, because it places all the emphasis on the Real Presence rather than the Sacrifice. I do not think it is accidental that while we speak naturally and habitually of a "Prayer of Consecration", a fourth-century bishop like St Sarapion calls his equivalent the "Prayer of Sacrifice," or "Oblation." I do not want to over-press that difference, but it is there. Our own usage is the result of a shift of emphasis. That is not necessarily bad, provided that we fully recognize the fact that there has been such a change, and do not confuse ourselves with the illusion that we are being "primitive." And the change does hinge to a great extent on the introduction of, or the quite different emphasis laid on, this idea of a "moment of consecration."

It is fashionable at the moment in some quarters to reprobate the whole notion of such a "moment," not always perhaps with a full understanding of what is involved. If the question be raised at all – and it seems a legitimate one – "Is there some part of the Eucharistic prayer, some statement, if you like, of its intention, which is *necessary* to that prayer, in the sense that without it the Church cannot guarantee that Eucharistic service as fulfilling her own idea of her own Sacrament?" – if that question be raised, the notions of a "formula of consecration" and a "moment of consecration" cannot be altogether excluded. The question was not directly raised anywhere in Christendom, at least not in that form, for a thousand years.

But the Western debates on Consecration and its effects were bound to raise it at some point. And when it was raised the West answered it (I cannot but think rightly) by making the norm of the Eucharistic prayer – the statement of intention in it without which she could not guarantee the Sacrament as her own – to lie in conformity to the Evangelical model, in the inclusion of the "Words of Institution." This was in accordance with the great bulk, though not the whole, of patristic practice, and, I would venture to say, of patristic *obiter dicta*. It was also the only answer possible in view of the actual wording of the Roman Canon, virtually the only Eucharistic prayer then in use in the West. (There were still other prayers on the fringes, in Sicily, Spain and perhaps some Celtic churches.)

This answer, of course, involves the whole question of the Epiclesis, both as between Rome and the East, and between our own *Book of Common Prayer* and the unnecessarily "foreign" proposals of 1928.[1] (We have our own tradition on Consecration which has held for thirteen centuries, ever since England was a Christian country. It is both useless and provocative to try to run counter to that.) The Latin Church quite certainly had not the Eastern practice in view in coming to its own conclusion. Equally the Byzantines only began to make a controversial point of the Epiclesis against the Latins much later, after the treacherous seizure of Constantinople by the fourth Crusade had permanently embittered relations between the Churches. I do not want to go into the question of the Epiclesis here from this point of view at all. Let us look at this question of a "formula" and a "moment" of Consecration rather more broadly:

As a contrast to our accepted Western view of it, here is a very early Eastern statement on the process and effect of Consecration: "The bread is hallowed by the power of the Name, and is not the same as it appeared to be when it was received, but it has been transformed by power into Spiritual power." (*Excerpta Theodoti*, 82.1) That is from Clement of Alexandria citing an earlier writer. You might date it originally about A.D. 160.

I had better explain first what he means by "hallowed by the power of the Name." The early Christians did not speak of "consecrating" the Eucharist as a rule, but of "Eucharistizing" it, or of "making Eucharist" to God. They did not bless the bread and wine, they blessed *God*. The Christian Eucharistic prayer seems to be originally a direct development from an old Jewish form of prayer, the *barakah*. This had three parts: (1) It blessed God for special mercies in the past, mercies which encouraged the faith that God would now grant

(2) the petition now made. In the Christian *eucharistia* (the word is a mere translation of the Hebrew *barakah*) the chief special mercies for which God was blessed were the Redemption and the Institution of the Eucharist, the latter especially justifying the expectation that God would now grant the petition for communion and its fruits, which followed. Both *barakah* and *eucharistia* alike ended with (3) what the Jews called a "Glorifying of the Name" of God, *i.e.* a doxology, to which both Jews and Christians attached the greatest importance. Thus Rabbi Judah the Prince declared that a *barakah* which did not include this "does not bless"; while St Hippolytus, *c.* A.D. 215, lays it down that every Christian *eucharistia must* end with a Trinitarian doxology, of which he gives the form (*Apostolic Tradition*, 6.4).[A] It is to this very important invocation of "the Name" of God in the final doxology that our passage from Clement refers.

This is a way of regarding Consecration very different from our own. The doxology here has become a formula for charging the elements with a mysterious efficacy. What is noticeable is that the whole process can be stated, as it is here, without any explicit reference to the Redemption in Christ at all. It is divorced from, or certainly not directly connected with, the Incarnation, even though we may assume that to be latent in the writer's thought.

Put beside this what is, I believe, the oldest epiclesis-form extant, that in the Liturgy of *Addai and Mari*. This rite is at the opposite pole from our Western ideas, in that it originally did not contain the Words of Institution at all, and in its oldest recoverable form it never once refers to the Body and Blood of Christ in any connection. Here is what, for want of a more exact term, I must call its "Consecration formula": "May there come, O my Lord, Thine Holy Spirit and rest upon this offering of Thy servants and bless it and hallow it, that it be to us for the pardon of offences and the remission of sins and for the great hope of resurrection from the dead and for new life in the kingdom of heaven." That is very beautiful as far as it goes. But again it does not connect the effect of Consecration with our Lord or his Redemption directly in any way.

I need not multiply instances; there is, very early (*c.* A.D. 115) that famous phrase of St Ignatius, that the Eucharist is the "drug of immortality, the medicine that we should not die," which is to be found in more than one Eastern Liturgy, and is probably a quotation by Ignatius from the Antiochene rite of his day. Or there is that "language of fear," ever recurring in the Eastern rites, which begins in the fourth century, and which habitually refers to the consecrated elements as "fearful," "most terrifying," *in themselves*.[B] That is something quite unknown in the Western rites.

Now, it is very easy, and perhaps rather cheap, to talk of "magic" in discussing such ideas. For my own part, I find too much in the New Testament concerning such things as the efficacy of "Prayer in the Name," or the disastrous physical effects of unworthy communions, to feel comfortable about the question-begging charges of that kind. But I think we shall all agree that this way of regarding Consecration and its effects does miss something of the fullness of the New Testament insistence that the Eucharist is primarily and essentially "the *anamnesis* (*i.e.*, 'recalling, the making present again') of *Me*." It is the Incarnate, the whole Christ, of Bethlehem, Calvary, Easter and Ascension – the *Redeemer*, in his adorable humanity hypostatically united to his Godhead – Jesus of Nazareth, Son of God and Son of Mary, who is present in the consecrated Eucharist, and in his humanity now present in this world *only* by the consecrated Eucharist.[C]

If the Eucharist be the extension of the Incarnation, then he who came into this world "to give his life a ransom for many" is present in the Eucharist *for* Sacrifice.

I would suggest to you that Sacrifice is a conception it is better to approach first from the point of view of the whole rather than of the parts. It has more than one essential part without which there is no sacrifice. But none of the parts gives it full meaning outside the context of the whole. Our Reformers laid the whole emphasis on Communion; it was then a neglected part, and they had some justification for what they did. But the result was an impoverishment and a distortion of Eucharistic theology from which we are still suffering. The Oxford Movement emphasized afresh the Consecration, again the remedying of a neglect. Yet again this has not left us with a balanced theology. And today there seems to be some danger that some supporters of the "Liturgical Movement" amongst us will over-emphasize the neglected Offertory, with its sociological implications, and the offering of "ourselves, our souls and bodies." Theology ought not to depend on a swing of the pendulum like that.

It is the whole Christ, the Incarnate Redeemer, who is present and acting in the Eucharist, acting as Incarnate, *by Sacrifice*, for our redemption. Sacrifice comes first; the Consecration and the Presence must be viewed primarily as effecting the *reality of the Sacrifice*, the Sacrifice by Christ of himself, and in him of all his members. The Western development, with its insistence on Consecration and the Presence rather than Sacrifice, has admittedly been somewhat one-

sided. But it has one saving feature. By its very binding of the Consecration so closely to the Words of Institution, it has never altogether
obscured the dependence of the Eucharistic sacrifice on the Personal
Redeeming Sacrifice of the Incarnate, as some other developments,
ancient and modern, have tended to do. With all its limitations, even
in its most extreme medieval forms, when the insistence on Consecration was at its strongest, it has never been in any danger of regarding
the Eucharist merely as the charging of the elements by consecration
with a spiritual power *of their own*, to be released for the communicant by consumption.

Let me end with the first Western statement on Consecration, by St
Justin of Rome, *c.* A.D. 150. It is well known, but it puts the matter
with a classic precision: "We do not receive this as common bread or
common drink. But *as by the Word of God Jesus our Saviour was
incarnate and took flesh and blood for our salvation*, so, we have
been taught, this food – whereof our blood and flesh by assimila-
tion are nourished – this food 'eucharistized' by a word of prayer
which comes from him, is the Flesh and Blood of that same Jesus
who was made Flesh. For the Apostles in their 'Memoirs' which are
called 'Gospels' have handed down that thus it was commanded them
(to do): that Jesus took bread and 'eucharistized' and said: 'Do this
for the *anamnesis* (recalling) of me; This is my Body.' And likewise
he took the cup and 'eucharistized' and said: 'This is my Blood'"
(*Apology*, 1.66).

There, in the first post-apostolic theologian of the Christian
Church, you have the root of the matter. All else is commentary.

(*TL* 106–13)


## Notes

A. I do not want to suggest that our own "Consecration Prayer" would have
been held "invalid" in the second century by reason of its lack of doxology,
because they did not think then quite along those lines; though they certainly
would not have liked it. Our prayer does not really conform to any of their
desiderata; what it concentrates on are just those things, and only those things,
which later mediaeval theology thought important in eucharistic doctrine.

B. These examples do not, of course, represent the whole of Eastern teaching
on the eucharist, though it is quite certainly a persistent strain in that teaching.
And, so far as the extant evidence carries us, it would appear to be earlier in
development than those fourth-century and, from our standpoint, more normal
presentations of that teaching in Chrysostom, Cyril of Jerusalem and others,
who have moulded subsequent Eastern theology. Even so, I think the effects and

traces of this earlier Eastern tradition are at times visible even in Chrysostom, Cyril and, above all, Ephrem the Syrian, hampering the development of their own theology. I should regard the later Eastern view (and rite) as an insecure compromise between an ancient doctrine which regarded what is received in the eucharist as "Spirit," in a rather special sense which has no exact reference to the Holy Spirit (a view which comes ultimately from Semitic Christianity), and the more normal Hellenistic (Pauline) doctrine of the Body and Blood. One would expect to find the compromise develop first just where one does find it, in Greek Syria in the fourth century. The question of the Epiclesis, quite apart from the rather dull later controversial issues between Greeks and Latins, does ultimately open up some fascinating questions on the different religious psychologies of Semitic and Hellenistic Christianities in early days.

C. This is the theological justification of extra-liturgical devotions. If we now would find Jesus of Nazareth externally *present*, it is there that we must go. Extra-liturgical devotions may or may not be a good thing. But those who argue against them on the ground of the omnipresence of Jesus are merely the victims of that inveterate tendency of pietism to evacuate the reality of the humanity of Jesus, confusing and confounding it with the nature of Godhead.

1. What Dix considers 'foreign' is the position of the epiclesis after the institution narrative in the Eucharistic prayer, a characteristic feature of the Eastern liturgical tradition.

## Lammas Day – an Italian Harvest Festival

*Dix wrote this letter to the Revd William Norris, Vicar of St Margaret's, Leigh-on-Sea, and an oblate of Nashdom, in response to a query on the liturgical origins and subsequent observance of Lammas Day (1 August).*

18 August 1944

Dear Reverend Father

Thank you for your letter. I have been occupied with a retreat or I would have answered before. I apologise for the delay.

I think it is certain from the evidence of St Aldhelm and Egbert of York and Bede that St Augustine introduced at Canterbury the Roman *Gregorian Sacramentary* in which 1st August is *St Peter ad Vincula*. Most of the Anglo-Saxon calendars contain only this entry. But some of the eighth and ninth century ones, especially those from the north of England, have a number of entries not found in the *Gregorian*. Among these is 1st August: *Passio Macchabeorum*. This is the alternative feast of that day found in the south Italian

*Gelasian Sacramentary.* There is a strong south Italian strain in the early Northumbrian liturgical books. For example, some of them reproduce the Neapolitan not the Roman Gospel lectionary (and one of them the Capuan Gospel lectionary). Probably this derives from two sources: (a) The Frankish church in the seventh, perhaps even the sixth, century was using the *Gelasian Sacramentary*, a 'south Italian' edition of the current 'pre-Gregorian' Roman rite, and some of the Frankish sacramentaries got across the channel in the eighth to ninth centuries. (b) Benedict Biscop in his three voyages to Rome bought a number of Italian manuscripts for the library of Wearmouth-Jarrow, and some of these books were of 'Italian' and not *local* Roman origin (probably he found them in the 'second-hand bookshops' of Rome). Among them, for example, is *Codex Amiatinus* of the Gospels. The importance of Jarrow-Wearmouth as a copying centre in the North ensured a wider distribution for their texts than might have been expected. But so far as I know, by the tenth century the large majority of Anglo-Saxon calendars have either only St Peter on 1st August or have St Peter with a commemoration of Ss Macchabees. By the eleventh century this is practically universal, and was the Canterbury use – or that of the Archbishop himself, anyhow – as found in the missal of Robert of Jumièges, Archbishop in 1051 A.D.

I know of *no* Anglo-Saxon calendar which calls 1st August Lammas Day. So far as I know there was never a *mass* of 'Lammas'. The blessing of a loaf at mass on 1st August like the blessing of grapes on 6th August (older than Transfiguration which is a mediaeval French invention) is of Italian origin and was done with a collect only, either before mass began or at the end of the canon. It is, of course, the Italian equivalent of the harvest festival – the 'blessing of first fruits'. Even allowing for the difference of nearly a week due to the maladjustment of the Julian calendar by *circa* 1000 A.D., there would be few years in England in which harvest was *over* by 1st August. But the Italian grain harvest begins early in July. The rather mechanical adoption of the Italian observance in Anglo-Saxon churches perpetuated this little ceremony in mediaeval England, but it was too pointless here ever to become more than a special little addendum to the ecclesiastical rite on that day in England. It was never a holiday. But it was a customary day for hiring labourers before the *beginning* of the grain harvest in this country. Hence its perpetuation in the Elizabethan calendar. I think it was only called 'Lammas' by the population to distinguish it from the chief feast of the apostle on 29th June. The emphasis laid on this aspect of 1st August by some modern Anglican liturgists seems to be a modern invention, not based on authentic tradition at all.

I cannot trace the mass you give for 'loaf-mass' in any English source at all, but I have not looked in the *Leofric Missal*, not having the text at hand. It might be there, but the *Leofric Collector* gives only *S Petri ad Vincula*. The collect looks to me a modern invention.

The feast of 1st August originated certainly as the dedication feast of the Church on the Esquiline, but I rather suspect as the fourth century dedication feast of the original church, not the fifth century restoration by Eudoxia. What gave it 'interest' outside the parish was the relic of the chains which had a great reputation for cases of demoniac possession. Eudoxia appears to have brought these from Jerusalem – the great factory of such things in the fifth century. Their repute increased steadily from the sixth century to the tenth, and with this the feast is more and more widely observed as time goes on. (It is always relics which spread the observance of feasts in this period). The Gallican rite proper was in full decay by the eighth century, and in decline by the seventh – *i.e.* new texts for feasts were no longer being composed in those churches in the south of France which still kept up the Gallican rite and had not yet adopted the Roman. But the sister-rite of Spain (Mozarabic) which had not yet fossilised was already ousting the old Spanish feast of St Felix on 1st August at Cordova in the calendar of 961 A.D. The feast was certainly kept in *some* French churches in the ninth century but with the Roman rite.

Mother Lucy seems a bit of a tartar by all accounts!

Yours sincerely *in Dño*

Gr. Dix O.S.B. (with renewed apologies for the delay)

# Part Two

# Shaping the Spiritual Life

# The Image and Likeness of God

*Although preached to two communities of sisters (the Community of the Holy Name, Malvern Link, and the Community of the Sisters of the Church, then at South Wraxall, Wiltshire) and once to a priests' retreat at the Mission House, Cowley, the scope of these addresses, inspired by 1 Corinthians and based on the theology of Bernard of Clairvaux, extends far beyond the spiritual needs and interests of religious and clergy. Indeed, such are their insight and depth that Dix's friend and Abbot, Dom Augustine Morris, edited them for posthumous publication in 1953, in a volume entitled* The Image and Likeness of God.*

## The Image of God

The Bible is full of expressions about the littleness and wickedness and weakness of man, his comparative insignificance in nature. Yet the Bible for all that never treats man as just a part of nature on a level with the rest, never regards either his weakness or his wickedness as a sign of insignificance. On the contrary, the Bible is nothing else but the story of the absolute and eternal significance of man, of each single man, to the everlasting God. Not indeed that he is significant in himself, but only in relation to God; for, as St. Paul says, every man, any man, is "the image and glory of God." (1 Cor. 11.7)

Man, says the Bible, was made "in the image and likeness" of God. (Gen. 1.26) Whereas the rest of the created universe in a measure reflects the goodness and beauty of God, yet of man alone is it said that he was made in God's image: and in that little sentence is contained all the glory of man and all the possibility of tragedy in man . . .

Man is, and is conscious of being, something which all the material universe put together is not and cannot be – a *person*, a self-directed being. Within certain limits, he can choose his own "ends", direct his own life, decide upon his own objectives: and this he does from *within* his own being. True, this freedom has certain limits . . . But within these various limits, I have a very considerable degree of freedom . . . to decide what I shall make of my manhood. Though mysteriously unable fully to achieve them, I can *choose my ideals.*

Yet, although a free being, I remain a *created* being, dependent for my very existence upon what is outside myself, dependent upon my parents for the gift of my body, and upon God for the gift of my soul. This is indeed the deep mystery of my being, that I am at once both *created* and *free.* The whole tragic possibility of sin lies here. I am able of my own nature to go against the very Being of That upon Which I am utterly dependent – and yet I do not immediately destroy myself in so doing. This is the painful mystery of man's existence.

How comes man to be in this strange position, a creature of two worlds, at once a mere fragment of physical nature and yet able to rise altogether above it through this dangerous gift of freedom? . . . The reason, the all-sufficient reason, lies in the singular dignity of being made in the image and likeness of God.

God is a Personal God. "God is love", holy love. The love of God does not mean that He is subject to emotion, or that His love is liable, like ours, to wane or increase or to get out of control: rather it expresses the deep sovereign purpose, all-mastering, all-powerful of Holiness in Personality: of utter infinite Holiness in unlimited Personality. Man is the creature of Love, made for Love's purpose. And that purpose is the *return* of love . . .

Whereas we can *know* the universe, we cannot in the same way know God. The universe, however great, is finite. But "God dwelleth in light inaccessible." (1 Tim. 6.16) "No-one hath seen God at any time." (John 1.18) The Bible is very sure that we can *never* adequately comprehend God, just because He is infinite. Our power fails there: the instrument is insufficient. We cannot know Him as He is, though we can have a sufficient knowledge of Him to love Him. We cannot know *what* He is, all that He is exhaustively, but we can know *that* He is, and we do experience the effects of His Being; and these things are wholly sufficient to move us to love Him, and thus to be filled with all the fullness of Him.

(*ILG* 17–22)

## The Image Defiled

There lies in the very nature of man as created by God the possibility of darkest tragedy. God has made man in His own image, and that involves above all the power of love: and in order to love at all, man must be free. In order to love at all, he must be free to refuse love, and free also to love the wrong object. He chooses of his own accord how he will use this power of love, which is his greatest glory. Just here lies the possibility of sin, in the fact that man is a creature, subject on the one hand to the law of his being, a law not of his own making, and yet free on the other hand to obey that law or break it.

In fact, man has used that freedom by breaking the law of his being. He not only can sin, but he has sinned and does sin, and you and I and everyone are involved in the consequences of that sin. Once sin has entered into the world, its results are inevitably disastrous. We have to face the terrible and tragic fact of original sin, with all the disasters it brought upon the human race . . . You and I have inherited human nature, with its wonderful powers of knowing, and loving, and its freedom, by which it is the image of God, but the nature we have inherited is disrupted by sin . . . The image of God in us, our very freedom, has been spoilt by sin before we have received it. There is now a dolorous and disastrous contrast and opposition between man, made in the image of God, and God his Maker, the Original of the image . . .

Man – it is the experience of every one of us – is no longer altogether free to be his true self, the complete Image of God. For him, now that sin has entered into the world, life is a perpetual struggle against desires and temptations, just because his free will is damaged by sin. He can indeed win the struggle, with the help of God's grace – but only with the help of God's grace. Even so, *some* sin is inevitable. Not indeed that any particular sin is inevitable, or any particular temptation overwhelming; but yet sin at some point or other is inevitable. "We have all sinned", says St. Paul, "and come short of the glory of God" (Rom. 3.23), of that glory which the "image of God" should mirror exactly, though in miniature.

The *possibility* of sin lies therefore in the combination of creatureliness and freedom: the *fact* of sin lies in the abuse of the freedom of the creature by wrong and evil choice. Man can sin in either of two ways: by exaggerating and abusing his freedom, or by minimising it and exaggerating and abusing his creatureliness.

He can exaggerate his freedom by forgetting or trying to forget that he is a creature subject to the law of God. He succumbs to the temptation of the devil, "Ye shall be as gods" (Gen. 3.5), choosing for yourselves what you will call your good and what your evil . . .

Or else man can exaggerate his creatureliness and try to run away from his freedom. He can insist that he is only a creature on the same level with other creatures, and that he cannot and will not be responsible for what he makes of his life. He abdicates his freedom and plunges into sensuality. The animal desires of his own nature gain the mastery of him, not he of them. And through these desires the *things* which are the objects of his desire become his masters . . .

Sin is spiritual death, death to man's true being, because it destroys the divine image in the soul. The malice of sin lies here. It is true that sin disrupts man's own inner harmony. But what is infinitely worse is that it strikes at God so far as it can reach Him: it as a sort of deicide. It attempts to blot Him out of His own universe. He is unassailable *there*, but He has exposed Himself to assault in that "little world" which lies within man. That is why Satan is so eager to lead us into sin, for he can thus strike at God and outrage Him in His own image. In this way only can the devil make effective assault upon God.

"If we say that we have no sin we deceive ourselves. But if we confess our sins He is faithful and just to forgive us our sins." (1 John 1.8-9) The recognition of our sinfulness is the essential prerequisite for the renewal of the image of God within our souls.

(*ILG* 24–8)


## The Image Restored

Consider what it is to be very God and very Man, God of God and Man of Man, representative man. It is to be at one and the same time infinite holiness and the capital representative of a sinful race. True, personally, He is sinless and guiltless. Yet it is of a sinful humanity that He is truly a member, and still more the head. "God made Him to be sin for us, Who knew no sin." (2 Cor. 5.21) In Him the Godhead and a sinful race are combined in hypostatic union! This is the bitter contradiction which is in Him, nay, which He *is*.

There is an absolute opposition there which cannot endure, which cannot find an equilibrium, which must tear Him apart to find its own resolution. "The wages of sin is death" (Rom. 6.23), and the sinful humanity which finds its Head in Him *must* die for sin. "Thine Almighty Word leaped down out of Thy royal throne . . . and filled all things with death." (Wisdom 18.15) He, the Word and Truth of God, *is* that death to the sinfulness of manhood as He enters humanity: He carries it in Himself in bearing our nature, even though He is come "that they may have life." (John 10.10) And because He is representative Man, the *Head* of the race, because He has come to redeem that sinful race from *within* that sinful race itself, from within the communion of sinners, it is necessary that that death to sinful humanity must strike at Him chiefly and first. Death looms up out of the primeval depths of human history as the great consequence of original sin confronted by the holiness of God. In Him the holiness of God is actually incarnate in human history in all its wicked reality. In Him the two opposites are not merely confronted but, as it were, combined. In Him the holiness of God thrusts itself into the very heart of the opposed reality. No wonder then that He asked the two disciples on the road of Emmaus, "*Ought* not the Christ to suffer these things?" (Luke 24.26) Calvary is the logic of the situation . . .

By this ultimate obedience of Love the perfect image of God has been borne unbroken, unbesmirched to the end. As yet, however, it has been brought back only into one single human life: we still have to see how it is to be renewed again in all men. The first Adam, the first man although a living soul yet of the earth earthy, transmitted the marred image by generation. The Second Adam, the second Man, is the Lord from Heaven, and He becomes quickening Spirit in the children of men. "As we have borne the image of the earthy", says St Paul, "we shall also bear the image of the heavenly." (1 Cor. 15.45–46)

The whole image of God is seen in Jesus Christ. He fulfils that law which from the beginning had been by God's disposition the law of human life – the law of love. "The image of the invisible God" is now enshrined in human life, an image truly filled with all the fullness of God. If we are to be renewed according to the image and pattern by which we were made, if we, as far as we are capable of such a thing, are to be filled with all that fullness, it can only be by sharing with Him and in Him. And so it is that St Paul sets forth as the means to that fulfilling, our realisation of the love of Christ, "that ye may know the love of Christ which passeth knowledge" and so "be filled with all the fullness of God." (Eph. 3.19)

(*ILG* 39–42)

## The Image Perpetuated

We come now to the Mass, that act of the Body of Christ in which even in time we do for a brief moment effectually "become what we are": children of God, His accepted sons and daughters, "accepted in the Beloved" (Eph. 1.6); members of Christ, living with His risen and ascended life in us, loving with His love in us; inheritors in the present, not merely heirs in the future, of the kingdom of God, "having become partakers of the inheritance of the saints in light" (Col. 1.12), and in union with God. In the Mass we do indeed "know the love of God which passes knowledge and are filled with all the fullness of God." ...

In Calvary as in the Mass, Jesus becomes what He is – Priest and Victim. Not indeed in His case, as in that of the baptized Christian, is there need for overcoming sin from *within* self as we must, in order that we may become what we are. Yet in Calvary He effectively becomes what He has been from the beginning of His incarnate life: Jesus, Saviour. And in the Mass He becomes *to us* what He is as Saviour, Priest and Victim for sin. The Mass is the necessary extension in place and time of Calvary. In the Mass also the church becomes what she is, the Body of Christ, and the Christian becomes what he or she is, a member of that Body ...

In the Mass we offer Christ, and with Him ourselves. We receive back ourselves, but transformed into Him. We receive back ourselves as members incorporated into Him and into His church. What we receive was of our own offering, but also of the offering of all our brethren as well. Through *their* giving our self-giving comes back to us: but above all the self-sacrificial love of Christ takes both us and them up and sacrifices us and renews itself in us. It is not we that bring Him down to us; rather He lifts us up to Him. Nor does our littleness cramp His greatness: rather His greatness expands us to His stature ...

We want to give ourselves to Him. But there is a truth of far greater importance than that: He longs to give Himself to us. When we speak of "*my* communion" we are really putting things the wrong way round: *His* communion with us is far, far more important. And so the reason for coming to Holy Communion is not really so much our need for Him, though that need is so dire that we perish without Him, but rather that *He wants us.* He loves us to the uttermost, He died for us, He has the right to what He wants from us – and so we go.

We go, and are taken up by Him into His self-sacrificial love. As St Augustine beautifully says of the Apostles, "They were of the poor who 'ate and were satisfied' (Ps. 21.27), because they suffered the same things as they ate. He gave His supper, He gave His passion: that disciple is satisfied in His supper who imitates Him in His passion." Our life is made a sacrifice to God, because it is made one with His sacrifice: we become what we are, members of Christ and images of God . . .

The offering of the Mass is the offering of the *whole* Church. The obligation of Sunday attendance at Mass is too often thought of as an individual obligation merely. But it is more than that. The real reason for it is the unity of the whole body, the need for all the members of the body to come together, the *one* body offering itself. The voluntary absence of one member spoils the offering of all the others corporately united, for the gift of all is not complete with the gift of each. So it is not just that *I* ought to receive Holy Communion once a week, or worship God once a week by attendance at Mass, but rather, I ought to give myself to and with the others in the corporate worship of the whole body.

The church, His Body, because it is His Body, is the image of God. We as members of that Body share that image and worship and suffer and work as members of that Body and sharers of that image. "We bear about in our body the dying of the Lord Jesus, that the life also of Jesus might be made manifest in our body." (2 Cor. 4.10) That dying and that life are eternal facts, and they are perpetuated in time and realised in the lives of Christians through the Mass. In His sacrifice, consummated on Calvary and perpetuated in the Mass, our puny efforts to offer ourselves, so often frustrated by our own shortcomings and sins, are yet precious in the eyes of God, Who there discerns the mark and image of His divine Son.

(*ILG* 51–2, 57–8, 61–2)

## The Power and Wisdom of God

*Taking his inspiration from St Paul's description of Christ as 'the power of God and the wisdom of God' (1 Cor. 1.24), Dix broadcast six Holy Week addresses on the BBC Home Service in 1948. To be given an opportunity such as this is evidence of Dix's popular appeal as a preacher, and the talks themselves provide a valuable insight into his understanding of the passion and resurrection of Christ.*

### The difference Christ makes

Some people say 'I don't think it matters what people believe, provided they do what's right.' That simply is untrue, because it begs the whole question. What *is* 'right'? By and large – Conduct – what you do in real life – is three quarters of it the result of what you believe. If you believe – if you honestly and wholeheartedly believe that power over the lives of your fellow men and women is the most worthwhile thing in life – then consciously or unconsciously it is going to affect nearly everything you do, and the way you do it, and why you do it, and you in the doing of it. You will give up a lot of your time and the best of your energy and much of your thought to gaining and trying to exercise your power over others. That is what you really persistently want. If you succeed, you will probably make life a hell for some of them. You will be an ambitious man, you will become an unscrupulous man, you will probably end up as a cruel man – because power is the most corrupting of all temptations.

Or if you believe that security – financial security or social security or physical security, all sorts of security – is the most worth-while thing in human life, you will probably have a pretty worrying time of it, as things are. Or if you believe that ease and comfort for yourself is the real end of life, to be procured for yourself at all costs to yourself or others, then you will become a lazy, selfish man. And so on. It depends what is the chief end or purpose which you put before yourself in living your life. Perhaps it isn't as deliberate as that – the chief end or purpose for which you do as a matter of fact live and act and choose, most of the time. Yet it is a matter of what you *believe* is most worth-while. That affects everything you do and the way you do it.

But if you believe that the real end and purpose of living your ordinary life is something *outside* human life altogether – that it lies somehow in God – then that also is going to affect everything you do, and the way you do it and you in the doing of it. Truly to seek God – most people want to do that some time or another. The trouble is 'How to set about it' and that I seem so often and so soon to get in my own way – and then there are other people and circumstances. Yet Christians want it permanently – I don't mean all the time, but with the general set and direction of their lives. We can and do waver a good deal and go off after other things, sometimes very hard, for a long time. But that is what at the very bottom of our wills we would 'like to want', steadily and all the time, if I may put it like that.

In fact, if we sincerely believe that the main end and purpose of human life lies in seeking and finding God, we come at once to the question of sin and goodness. God, we know, is sheer *goodness* – without flaw and without alloy. All our deepest instincts tell us that. And all the men who have most ceaselessly sought Him and found

Him – the prophets and saints – have found Him so. They tell us that. And if we do set out to seek Him – we soon find it so, too. We can soon tell ourselves that. And there is something unbearable as well as infinitely desirable in the burning, unvarying, immeasurable goodness of God, without end, for ever and ever. It is there – all that I can most desire – the goodness without shadow, the truth without doubt or question, beauty beyond all wearying – but though I may desire it, I know that I am unfit, totally unfit, for it, even if I attain to it. I may want goodness, but there is that in me which repels it. Sin is as real in me, when I look into my own heart, as goodness is real to God. What is to be done about that? What can I do about that? Is the desire for God just a beautiful mirage, something I must just give up because it is not for me, at all events?

It is the heart and core of the Christian Gospel that something has been done about it – that in the life, death and resurrection of Jesus of Nazareth, God has *acted* about sin. 'Christ died for our sins and rose again for our justification' – rose from the dead on the third day to become goodness in us.

(*PWG* 1–4)

## God's Loving Initiative

There is a great 'toughness' about the Christian claim that Christ crucified is the Power of God and the Wisdom of God mastering the world, which enables the Church to survive catastrophes which destroy everything else. Yet externally the Church is only a society of sinful, imperfect, short-sighted men and women, suffering the pressures of history just like everyone else, perhaps even more than most. What makes the difference is that the Church is the Society which accepts and lives by that claim, that 'God was in Christ reconciling the world to Himself.'

Why should we put it that way round? Surely it was the world that had sinned and God who was outraged? Surely there is a dumb desire for God always at the heart of the world. Ought we not to say that Christ by offering Himself to God from within the sinful world reconciled God to the world? A good deal of Christian thinking, especially since the sixteenth century, has put it that way, and you can if you like. But that way you are apt to miss the point that 'God so loved the world' in spite of its sin 'that He gave His only begotten Son'. It always was God's world, even in sin. He had made it out of love, and He would save it out of that abiding love. 'He came unto *His own*' . . . that is the chief emphasis of the New Testament. The motive lies all the time in God Himself, in His own nature and being, His lovingness – not in the world's loveliness, which came from God; nor yet the world's need, which is the fruit of its sin. It is God's love which reconciles. That is the permanent, positive thing. It is sin which opposes reconciliation, and repels the love of God, for sin cannot exist in Him. That is how sin asserts itself, by repelling God's love. At the root of all sin is always the distorted self-assertion, the incessant return upon self to the exclusion of God. That is the pitiful cry of the Prince of this world as he fell: 'I am God. I will sit in the seat of God in the heart of the seas.' It is his first whispered promise to humanity, by which we have all fallen: 'Ye shall be as Gods' – dying rivals to the Living God. There is no room for Godhead here. 'His own received Him not.'

But how came the world to be in need of reconciling? By what weakness or folly had God let it slip from His arms? Again the whole motive lies in God's own being – in His love. It was through the permanent weakness of love, which to the proud eyes of sin always looks like folly. The Lover had to *trust* the Beloved. It is the very nature of love to long for, to seek a return of love. But that return must be freely given. In every impulse of love there is always an act of trust, of trust that the Beloved will *freely* return love. Sometimes in men and women we do find a desire that is satisfied with an unfree return – and we call that not love but lust. Of a God who could contrive an unfree return of love from a free creature, a God who was content with an automatic sanctity in men and women, we should have to write the dreadful text 'God is lust', and then there would be nothing left but despair.

Men and women are made by and for the love of God; they are made for the free return of love to God. To love at all men and women must be free. And if they are to be truly free, they must be free to refuse love, even if in refusing they frustrate their own being. God seeks their love, but their choice must be real. It must come from within themselves. Even the torrent of God's love for them must never overwhelm that freedom. That is the risky logic of love. And God, the unrestrained lover – who is love – must act by it. So man is free, and man chose, and chooses – not the going forth from self in love, but its opposite – the return upon self, the sterility of self-assertion. That is the anatomy of sin. And long continuance and communication of sin has made it almost a second nature.

And the remedy? There cannot be a remedy that does not leave man free. The love of God cannot force, cannot terrify, man into returning love, without destroying itself as well as the very return it seeks. The love of God cannot even 'scrap' the free creature it loves and start again with another, unless the God who is everlasting love should cease to love.

It looks insoluble. But the power of God and the wisdom of God found a way – a way so powerful that only God could be trusted to do it, and so subtle that it needed a long preparation of man, if he was to understand and freely to accept it. That preparation is in the Old Testament and the long history of its records. Without that the Gospel could never have been, or been understood. God Himself, the Living God, would enter in person and without reserve into that vast network of seed and blood that binds all the human generations. From *within* that communion of sinners, through *their* freedom, God Himself would freely work out the return of humankind's love to God. Even God's entrance into humanity must be freely conceded. It depended on the consent of a woman. That is the glory of Mary the Virgin, that she alone ever *gave* to God, something that was not His by right – creaturehood. And so God came into the world, bone of our bone and flesh of our flesh, very Man, the son of His Mother. There was nothing unearthly about Him, nothing even remote from ordinary life, with all its freedom and all its sin. He is a man of His own time and place and He takes His full part in the life of His time and place. After thirty unspoilt years of quiet human preparation, He goes into politics – not even idealistic politics, but corrupt oriental politics, tortuous, murderous, vile. The man who would be Messiah in first century Palestine necessarily handled the most explosive problem in the whole Near East. With a conduct humanly skilful but totally innocent He threads His way through that whirlpool of human fear and hatred and pride and treachery and greed, until in the end all those representative human sins discharge their terrible consequences upon Him. He had foreseen that. He accepts all those consequences deliberately, willingly, lovingly, but never once deviates because of them from His own course, which is set fixedly by the love of God. As man He took all the consequences of those representative human sins upon Himself, and did not for one instant cease to love with the love of God.

(*PWG* 19–23)

## The Balance of Life

For people who accept it and take their own acceptance of it seriously, belief in the Atonement of Jesus Christ is bound to change the quality of their lives a good deal.

Let me begin by saying what I *don't* mean by that. I don't mean that every orthodox Christian automatically becomes an outstandingly noble character or even a specially attractive and pleasant person to live with. He doesn't. People are all different, and make themselves more different from each other as life goes on. At least, they should do so. When a man is converted, or when he enters consciously into his inherited Christian faith, he remains the same person that his heredity and his surroundings and his experiences and his previous choices and actions have already made him. The good points and the weak points of his character remain in him, acting and combining all the time to make him the particular person he is. That is always the material that the grace of God has to work upon. Even if a man surrenders himself and his life to the action of grace as completely as he knows how, grace will never destroy either his individuality or his freedom. A Christian is not meant to become merely another specimen of a machine-made pattern of sanctity completely identical in all its examples. St Peter never became at all like St John or like St Paul. On the contrary, St Peter seems to have become more and more like St Peter, and St John like St John, and St Paul like St Paul. That is what ought to happen. A man by grace ought to become actually more himself, more individual. By the grace of God the *consequences* of his defects and character may and should be prevented. But as a rule the particular traits in his character which apart from grace would have worked out as faults do not alter. And just because God's grace does not destroy a man's freedom but works with it and strengthens it, it should heighten and deepen the things in his character which make him *that* man, unlike everybody else. If he goes far in the life of grace, he will become *that* man perfected. But all the same, belief in the Atonement of Jesus Christ for his sins does alter the centre and balance of his life, and so alters the whole quality of it.

It alters its centre. The root of sin is self-regardingness, that perpetual return upon self, to the exclusion of God, which develops into all the things which spoil human life. We all know how much each of us tend all the time to think of 'myself' as the centre of all existence. We entrench ourselves, as it were, in the centre of the circle, and we think of everything and everybody else as the circumference. We like people and things, we welcome events, not so much for what they are in themselves as because they seem to give pleasure, comfort, profit, safety – some sort of satisfaction to *me*. We dislike or distrust people and things, we repel, threaten, attack them, we try to oppose events – just because and only because – we think they bring discomfort, displeasure, discredit to *me*. That is what I mean by making ourselves the centre of the circle. It seems so natural a way of looking at life, that we do it unconsciously all the time – without being aware most of the time how nonsensical such an attitude really is. After all, I am not really the centre of all existence. Things and people existed before me, and will exist after me. They would have existed though I had never been. We know as soon as we consider it that they don't exist only in relation to me. When we think it out, we acknowledge theoretically that they must exist, as I must exist, chiefly in relation to God who created them and me. Yet all the time we tend naturally to slip into the way of putting 'me' at the centre and everything else at the circumference, and living life *in practice* accordingly. It is quite fatally easy to treat even God that way – to regard Him chiefly as somebody whose principal business is to keep all the things I can't control for myself, going smoothly for me. We often pray very earnestly and sincerely things which must sound to the Holy Angels like 'MY will be done', much more than 'Thy will be done'. That is the natural tendency – to treat 'myself' all the time as the standard and centre of everything. God may have given me my being, but we take it for granted that that is about the most important thing He has done, and everything and everybody else revolves around that and for that. Push that unconscious principle just a little further – into action in daily life – and all the pride and fear and conceit and greed and hatred and lust and cruelty in human life is the result. That is what I mean by saying that self-regardingness, self-centredness, the return upon self all the time to exclusion of God, is the root of sin.

Now the man who really accepts the fact that Jesus Christ died for their sins cannot thoroughly do that. He knows like everyone else that he owes his own being to God. But he knows something more. He knows that all the time he *depends* for the *rightness* of his own being on God, on something that God did and does, something that he cannot conceivably do for himself. He is continually aware that God did not just start him off, so to speak, and leave him to his own importance. Not only his existence, but the rightness of that existence, is all the time dependent on the love and mercy and grace of God given in Jesus Christ. In other words, *God* becomes the centre of the circle and he himself, along with everything else, becomes part of the circumference. That alters the centre of his life. It is bound to affect the quality of it.

(*PWG* 25–8)

## Easter Communion

The last thing Jesus did before He went out to die was to fix the meaning of His death and of what was to follow from it upon the minds of His followers, for ever, not perhaps in a way that they could grasp fully at the moment, but in a way they could not possibly help coming to understand later for themselves, with a meaning that would only deepen and deepen as the years went by. Two little sentences attached to the only two things they were quite certain to do again frequently and *to do together*. The Divine economy of the means, and the Divine security of it! 'This is My Body which is for you'. 'This is the New Covenant' of a new Israel 'in My Blood'. He imposed for ever upon the terrible scandal of His voluntary death on the morrow the character of a voluntary sacrifice for sin offered in His own Body and Blood by the High Priestly Christ Himself – the sacrifice of the Lamb of God that taketh away the sins of the world. And Christians have entered into that sacrifice ever since, by 'doing this for the re-calling of Him'. And 'He is known to them' all down the centuries 'in the breaking of bread'. In every age that is the source and the mani-festation and the realisation of the life of the Church, which St Paul calls 'the *fulfilment* of Him who is being fulfilled altogether in all' of us. The Church all down the centuries is the *result*, the 'fulfilment', of His death and resurrection.

You are going to your Easter Communion tomorrow. When you do that, remember that *you* are part of that *fulfilment*, part of that vast progress through the catastrophes which has now outlasted three great human civilisations and is in the process of outlasting another before our very eyes. When you take your Communion you too affirm that Christ died for *our* sins (mine amongst the rest) and rose again for our justification – to become goodness in us. 'As oft as ye do eat this bread and drink this cup ye do proclaim the Lord's death till He come' – not merely that He died, but that He died *as the Lord*, as the Christ offering Himself by the power and wisdom of God, in sacrifice, for the sins of the world. And what you receive is His life, His real life, through His Body and Blood – but a life that has passed through death for sin – your sin. He comes to be the death of sin and the life of goodness in you. That has to be taken seriously. The death of Christ is the measure of how seriously God takes your sins, how overwhelmingly He desires their abolition. Examine them, face them, detest them, renounce them. I believe that the right way is to confess them to God before a priest. At all events be sure to confess them to God before yourself. And then don't let their existence be an excuse for not communicating. You can go with a sure trust in Him Whom you will there receive. You do not bring down His divine greatness to your own littleness. He lifts you up into Himself. There He makes you one with Him, and one with the Saints and Angels who are already one with Him, one with the holy dead who died in the faith, one with each other, one with all who are His. It is in your Communion that He is displayed as your Redeemer, and that you take Him for your Lord and for your life. 'This is My Body which is for you.' 'This cup is the New Covenant in my Blood.' 'Christ crucified to them which are called the Power of God and the Wisdom of God.' I wish you a holy and happy Easter.

(*PWG* 45–7)

## God's Way with Man

*Three years after his Holy Week addresses were broadcast on the BBC, Dix was invited to lead the preaching of the Passion on Good Friday in the Church of the Resurrection, New York. In his foreword to these addresses, based on the Seven Last Words of Christ, published posthumously in 1954, Michael Ramsey notes that in Dix's last preaching of the Passion 'we seem to find an intense concentration of heart and mind upon the ultimate verities: Calvary's judgement upon Man, and Calvary's gift to him of selfless love evoking selfless love in return'.*

### Three Hours with Christ

When we come to spend three hours with our Redeemer while He carries the weight of the whole world's sins, the sin of all the men and women who ever have lived and ever will live, it is necessary to begin from the Apostolic understanding of the Gospel facts.

The facts themselves are so great and yet so simple, so deep and yet so bare, that it is easy enough to misunderstand them. The superficial mind can be baffled in interpreting them by their very simplicity and bareness, just as easily as the devout mind can misunderstand them from sentimentalizing them. There is no room for simplification or sentimentality about Calvary. You cannot make it appear ordinary and you cannot make it appear pretty. The facts themselves are gigantic, and they are terrible and they are in the last analysis joyful. They deal with the ultimate things in all existence, in God's existence as well as man's, though they deal with perfectly simple, concrete, individual things.

And God is loving, He is love itself, but He is never sentimental. He is the love which has no illusions whatever, and for that very reason is free to love triumphantly and unrestrainedly. He is the love that is absolute truth, that is true love – the love that vindicates itself simply by its own finality and absolute lack of self-interest. It has, therefore, no need to justify itself by appealing to anything outside to give it additional interest, or beauty, or force. It is that love of God for man, that sort of love of God for man, which expresses itself upon Calvary in the only way appropriate to a sinful world. That is what happens to love in the face of sin: love is crucified by its own objects. Calvary is the final expression in history, once and for all, of what God is like and what man is like apart from God. The only possible way of reconciliation must come from God's side; it cannot come from man's. Man can only accept it, and it is not until man *has* accepted it that he can understand it and take part in it . . .

Calvary, then, is not just a tragic and pathetic incident nineteen hundred years ago; a misunderstanding, a perversity of a comparatively few men – Pilate, Caiaphas, Judas, the mob – all long, long ago dead and condemned. Calvary is something which concerns every son of Adam and every daughter of Eve who shall ever live. It happened once for all in history, in real life, in naked flesh and blood fact; in that sense it is unrepeatable. There is only one Jesus of Nazareth, Son of Mary, and Son of God Most High, who offered Himself once as the Victim for sin and was once accepted. But Calvary is none the less the everlasting, the unwearying, unceasing love of God for the men and women he has created out of love, *permanently* in action for them. It is *my* sins and *my* deliverance from them and from myself, and *my* eternal salvation which is in question outside that gate upon that hillock on that afternoon. That is why we watch the action of God neither with absolute sorrow (for who can be finally sorrowful at his own deliverance?) nor yet with joy (for who can watch with joy the agony of his own Redeemer?). We watch with awe, and heartfelt gratitude, and trust, and penitence, and above all with adoration as God arises to the judgment of life and the final condemnation of all in life that is opposed to Love.

(GWM 15–17, 22–3)

## Father, forgive them

Calvary does indeed manifest the righteousness of God. It shows us how unfaltering the love of God *always* is, even while we sin. In the very act God still loves us. God detests the sin so much because it spiritually slays the sinner. But the sinner is the object of His love. All sin is an attempt to blot God out of His own universe, to act as though He were not there. But even while the sinner is striking at God's very face, God's love is still poured out on him. "Father, forgive them for they know not what they do". . . .

The answer to His prayer is jeers and mockery from every side. Jesus falls silent with the failure of His final example of Love. His patient endurance of it, the torturing wounds in hands and feet, the shame and ignominy and insult borne in silence are still a prayer to His Father, to whom He still commends all around Him. That silence sounds on down the centuries as words could not do, revealing in all its length and breadth and height and depth the abysses of the Love of God which are in Christ Jesus our Lord. You and I in our sins are included in that prayer, not by name, but by the fierce intentness of His Will that admits no complaint of His tortured body for itself. We are included and so is every other proud, and sensual, and greedy, and cruel, and ambitious, and cowardly, and slothful, and untruthful man or woman who ever lived or ever will live – if only they will let themselves be included. The goodness of God is like the unwearying, all-cleansing sea that washes all the coasts of the earth and receives without defilement all the pollutions that the land and the men upon it can impose.

Lord Jesus, pray for us, 'Father, forgive them for they know not what they do'. Pray this ever for us and for all poor sinners who will not pray it for themselves.

(GWM 27–8, 30–1)

## My God, my God

Now comes from the lips of the patient Jesus the most enigmatic and heart-rending cry in all the sorrowful history of mankind, "My God, my God, why hast Thou forsaken Me?" That He, so meek and yet so strong and so unswerving, should have had this agonized cry wrung from Him seems to have startled the soldiers . . . But for Him, what can it mean? We can never hope to plumb the whole depth of mystery that lies behind it. The spiritual agonies of the Passion – the final grappling with the iniquity of sin by the Holy Soul of Jesus – is some-thing we cannot hope to understand, because we are sinful and He, though tempted in all things as we are, was entirely sinless. We can only connect this dreadful inner conflict with the statement of St Paul, "God made him to be sin for us, who knew no sin; that we might be made the righteousness of God in Him". *To be sin!* We sinners cannot know what sin is in its deadly reality because it has become second nature to us. To be "The righteousness of God", overflowing, unend-ing, unvarying goodness of God; to "be made" the opposite of one's whole being, not from any attraction but as a helpless victim; to feel the cold death of the soul corroding one's innermost being, its slimy, polluting tentacles sliding and searching into all the spotless corners of the soul, while one loathes and hates it with all the righteousness and wrath of God – that is a horror we sinners can *never* suffer. But in some mysterious way, Jesus, the All-Holy, was subjected to it. That is what passes in the darkness of Calvary.

And with sin comes its fatal consequence – separation from God. God is the very Sun of souls. He gives warmth and light and life to them, even through their clouds and in their night. You and I have never seen that sun in all its splendour except, perhaps, in rare moments. The cloudless soul of Jesus has been irradiated by it, uninterruptedly, from the first moment of His being. But now the dark night of sin closes in around it as something utterly foreign and horrible, blotting out the light of His life, the full horror of it hid-den in the darkness around the Cross. We can only guess what that means. He is God of God, Very God of Very God, but He somehow takes upon Himself the torment of Hell: the loss of God, and the vision of God, and the hope of God. What would it mean to be shut up for ever in my own created nothingness? Shut in upon self, exclud-ing God?

There is no companionship in Hell. There is nothing but self-isolation and pride. In excluding Him, we exclude each other and all things. In God is all possibility of good, is all possibility of fulfilment; there is no good except from God. Apart from him there is no good. And in Hell there is the terrible knowledge that I have chosen this and *preferred* it. I have *made* myself like that! God always gives us the consequences of our own choice. And something of that hideous self-enclosure from the rejection of God is visited upon the innocent soul of Jesus on Calvary.

"My God, my God, why hast thou forsaken me?" Even there Jesus is faithful to the uttermost, though God seems to have betrayed and abandoned Him. But God is still God. He is still to be trusted. He is still called upon, and He is still proclaimed "*My God*", even though God seems to have abandoned Him. If He cried out in the words of Psalm 22, it would express the very horror of His seeming betrayal . . . But mark how the psalm ends . . . This is no cry of despair. It is a very song of triumph and exultation of the faithful soul that has actually experienced the faithfulness of God to His own.

(*GWM* 47, 49–55)

## I thirst

From one point of view this physical thirst of Jesus on the Cross is no mystery at all. It was always reckoned by the Romans as one of the worst sufferings of those who were condemned to be crucified that they experienced torments of thirst. We pass so lightly when we say the Creed over that phrase "*suffered* under Pontius Pilate". Every vein and artery in His whole Body cried aloud for moisture. He had told the woman of Samaria that He would give her "living water", that "whosoever drinketh of the water that I shall give him shall never thirst"; He had cried in the courts of the Temple, "If any man thirst let him come unto Me and drink"; He had taught in the synagogue of Capernaum that "He that believeth on Me shall never thirst." It was so true, the mockery of the Chief Priests: "He saved others, Himself He cannot save". That is always the predicament of love; it must give, give, give, all the time. It cannot do for itself what it must do for others. It cannot take to itself what it gives to others.

Only a few months before when James and John, the "Sons of Thunder", had pressed him to promise them the places on His right hand and left, He had asked them, "Can you drink of the cup that I drink of and be baptized with the baptism that I am baptized with?" And they had confidently answered that they could. He promised them that one day they should indeed drink of His cup of martyrdom and be baptized with the baptism of His Blood.

But first He must drink of it Himself. He had always thought of His coming Passion under these private mental symbols of a cup and a baptism. "I have a baptism to be baptized with: and how I am straitened till it be accomplished." I suppose it must go back in His mind to the baptism in Jordan and the heavens opened and His Father declared Him to be His beloved Son, and He was consecrated to be High Priest by the anointing of the Holy Ghost. He had seen then what manner of sacrifice He must offer. And then, the night before in Gethsemane: "Father, let this cup pass from Me, nevertheless, not My will but Thine be done." Now the baptism was upon Him; the cup is being drained to the dregs. And He surrenders Himself to the full human consequences of His sufferings.

Our Lord never pretends anywhere in the Gospels that suffering is an illusion or doesn't matter; that it isn't costly, and real, and frustrating to the human spirit. The sight of it always moved Him quickly to compassion, just because He knew its reality and its degradation of the best in man. So, simply and humbly and humanly He cries, "I thirst", and accepts the rough, awkward ministration that will relieve His need.

*(GWM 56–9)*

## It is finished

Our picture of Jesus on the Cross is of a Man, pale and weary, utterly exhausted, dying, brought there by an implacable enemy. From one point of view this is true. But if the King be Love, the Love of God, the Love that gives itself inexhaustibly, is not the triumph of love to give, and to give itself? He has given as none has ever given before Him, with all the prodigality of the unlimited God. He has given divinely – even within the limits and confines of human terms – so that He has actually manifested the righteousness of God which even the Holy Angels cannot look upon with unveiled faces. He has manifested it in the likeness of sinful flesh, in a creature, and in so doing He has delivered a lost world.

"It is finished" is the cry which sets the Cross, the tree of shame, the tree of death, the tree of defeat, in the very centre of human history as the Tree of Life, the Tree of Glory, the Tree of Victory, so that it is set upon the banners of kings. It is that in which we trust . . .

Satan's armour and weapons of self-interest had served him well enough to hold this world for his own palace and all men for his spoils. But Calvary has ended all that. The dying Jesus, piteous to see, humbling Himself to the death of the lowest criminal, looks like the "reject" of the world. He sees Himself as the conqueror of the world in the very manner and moment of His death, and that is how we Christians see Good Friday. It is no tragedy from our point of view, real and terrible though the conflict and agony were. It is not a defeat which is only lost to sight in the glorious recovery of Easter. Good Friday is itself the victory which Easter only proclaims. The end is accomplished upon Calvary, not in the garden around Joseph of Arimathea's sepulchre. Jesus – the stronger than the strong, the raider of the castle – makes ready to die, not as the vanquished in battle but as the final stroke of victory. This is the carrying of the inner gates of Satan's palace by storm. He takes from him all his armour and divides his spoil. "It is finished" – completed. The plan of God for human life is vindicated. Human redemption is achieved by the love of God from the hate of sin. Human suffering is given meaning and worth and dignity, raised from a mere frustration to be the very instrument of God's love and not its contradiction. It has been raised to that point by the nails driven through the hands and feet of God. Good Friday is no parade, no play-acting; the cost was real, the death was real, the Son of Mary was dead for three days. It is infinitely costly and therefore of infinite worth. "It is finished". Single-handed, at the cost of Himself, the Son of God, by becoming Son of Man, has triumphed in manhood for mankind by the human fact of death. We see Jesus made a little lower than the angels, for the suffering of death crowned with glory and honour, that He should taste of death for every man.

(GWM 65–8)

## He gave up the ghost

Death is a solemn and serious thing, even for those who are full of faith and are prepared to die. It should be a ritual act, an act of worship – a personal return of life to the God Who gave it – to the Lord of all life who is its fount, its master, and its end. It should be an act of solemn oblation and worship, an act of acknowledgement, an act of adoration, the pouring out of the whole being to Him whose rightfully it is. Supremely, it is an act of sacrifice to God.

I suppose we all of us think of death as, in some sense, necessary to sacrifice. It is not true; the essence of a sacrifice is not death. Wheat and oil, flour and salt were offered in temple sacrifices and involved no death. The essence of a sacrifice is *handing over to God* so that the one who sacrifices can never have it for himself again. For a living man, self-offered body and soul involves death and he knows it, and shrinks from it.

This final self-oblation Jesus now makes to His Father with utter serenity and self-abandonment. His trouble of soul, that separation from God, has now passed. His confidence in His Father was never more sure, more radiant. The victory is won. He is God's and He will now supremely acknowledge it. "Thou shalt love the Lord thy God with all thy heart and with all thy mind and with all thy soul and with all thy strength." His heart and mind will always be God's. Now, in these last three hours He has given all His strength. He has only to give His soul. "Father, into Thy hands I commend my spirit." You might translate it, quite literally and exactly, "Father, into Thy hands I will lay down from myself my spirit." It is the final self-oblation: not to be my own any more, but to be yours.

It is the total gift of oneself to the beloved that is the ideal of love, of human love in this life, and that is only a faint image of the total self-giving which is the Love of God. For ever in the Holy Trinity, the Father gives Himself to the Son and the Son to the Father in a torrent of love which is the Holy Ghost. The whole perfect Being of God passes eternally from one to another and returns in an unending dance of love – the perfect love of the perfect lover for the perfectly beloved, perfectly achieved and perfectly returned for ever. That is the life of God Himself in the eternal abyss of His own Being. It is love and it is joy, illimitable joy. Self-sacrifice in this world and the joy of God's own being are one and the same thing seen from different worlds. "These things have I spoken unto you that my joy might remain in you and your joy might be full". "Enter thou into the joy of thy Lord".

There is only one way: to let go of self, to give oneself to God out of love, the love that responds to His, manifested and demonstrated to the end on Calvary. "Herein is love, not that we love God, but that He first loved us." "Father, into thy hands I lay down from myself my spirit". *Father*, it is the first word of the first sentence he uttered from His Cross, and it is the first word of the last. All has been a giving up of Himself into God's hands.

"And having said thus He gave up the ghost."

(*GWM* 73–6)

## The Visitation of the Blessed Virgin Mary

*This is the first of three sermons transcribed from a handwritten note-book of ten sermons preached in 1945 and 1946. It was preached at the Patronal Festival of St Mary's, Slough on 8 July 1945 and, with minor alterations, on 7 July 1946 at Nashdom. In the Prayer Book calendar, the feast of the Visitation of the Blessed Virgin Mary is celebrated on 2 July. As an Anglo-Catholic, Dix's devotion to Mary is unsurprising. In this sermon, as in a number of his other writings, he makes much of Mary's unique role in freely giving to God the only thing that was not his by right – a human body.*

[Luke 1.36.] "This is the sixth month with her that is called barren. For no word of God shall be void of power" – the last words of the Angel at the Annunciation, the immediate prelude to the Visitation, your feast of title.

I think one of the real difficulties of leading the life of a Catholic Christian in our day is the great difficulty of relating our religious life in any very satisfying way to the surge and sweep of the mighty events which are passing daily before our eyes. You and I have lived through some of the most catastrophic and dramatic years in all human history. It happened by chance that on Friday afternoon I listened in to the hoisting of the Union Jack over Berlin. I suppose that in 1940 nine-tenths of the human race would have regarded that as hardly even a remote possibility within the next five years. We in this island may have dreamed of it occasionally, but how fantastic such an idea seemed even to us at that time. And now it has happened – and we have scarcely even taken note of it or been stirred by it.

Events have been so crowded and swift; so much which has happened is so unimaginable in its consequences for decades to come. It has all been so impersonally vast, so apparently uncontrollable by any sort of action that we individually could take, that we are numbed and bewildered. We seem to be in the grip of superhuman forces which bear each one of our tiny human destinies blindly and helplessly before them.

We do try to remember that if the Christian religion is true at all, then each single man and woman has an absolute and final importance which the greatest state and empire in its majestic history or its crashing fall can never really have at all. Each of these men and

women will be for ever the fit and rejoicing companion of an infinitely holy and beautiful and good God – men and women are rooted
in eternity. Earthly states and societies, even the greatest of them,
are rooted in time only, often only a very short time. How many
strong states have you and I seen overwhelmed in the last 40 years?
We do try – must try – to remember that human life has a meaning
far more significant and precious and true than the story told by the
bewildering chaos – or apparent chaos – of earthly history as we
see it unfolding before our eyes. The real divine meaning of human
living was told us once for all in the life of Jesus of Nazareth. We try
to remember that even the world we know is still God's world, that
He is its sovereign Lord and Lover, triumphant by effortlessly seeking
history and all that goes to make up history. But I think it is sometimes hard work to remember it in times like ours. We try to say our
prayers, to frequent the sacraments, to struggle with our own sordid
little temptations, we keep our fasts and festivals, and the round of
the Church's year. But it is apt to seem terribly irrelevant to "real life"
as it is happening here and now.

   And so we are in danger, we Christians, of living in two worlds
– a personal inner world, where the faith is still true, where we can
still say our prayers and kneel before the sacrament and find God in
Christ and be happy in Him – and then to step out of that into a real
world that is rather a nightmare, a world that even now is still at war,
and whose peace, such as it is, is haunted and hag-ridden with fear
and problems and cruelties almost past adding up.

   Is this a world in which it is any use – or in which we can even bear
– to think of the gracious idyll of the Visitation in the springtime
among the green hills of Judea, O so many centuries ago? When one
thinks of Belsen and Dachau or of Poland, what does it mean if a
young Jewish girl at the Annunciation *did* once take the kiss of God
and quicken with the embrace of the uncreated love that made the
world – in Galilee 1900 years ago? Even if she did go singing over the
hills to her cousin Elizabeth because she that was called barren was
also remembered of the Lord, and had the glory of giving life to the
last and greatest of the prophets, John the Baptist. Exquisite poetry,
no doubt! But even if it is true, thousands of her race have been put
to death with cyanide like rats – or suffered much worse fates – in
the last five years. And that is only our little facet of a tragedy almost
as wide as mankind, that has drowned the world in tears in our day,
perhaps deeper tears than ever before. Even if stories like the Visitation are true – or were true once – what can they have of meaning

for a time like ours? I think questionings like this come to many of us and they make our religion seem to us not so much "untrue" as irrelevant and "unreal".

Then the calm certainty of the word of the Angel who sent Mary to her Visitation of Elizabeth comes to us with a new and piercing meaning: "This is the sixth month with her that was called barren. For no word of God shall be void of power."

The world of our calamities is still somehow God's world. He still reigns in it, august and utterly holy, eternally secure, secretly and subtly and lovingly extracting by His most skilful power and goodness even from its most wicked sins and most blind perversities something of *good* which will even against the world's will, even without its knowledge, serve His ends of love. But when we are tempted to forget this, remember always that what the miseries and catastrophes of our own time have shown to be worthless is not this Christian certainty but the 19th century apostasy, the hope that the world apart from God could of itself and by itself save itself from the consequences of human sin. The old delusion that history could find some significance solely from within itself, that there was somehow some redemptive process at work in purely human history and endeavours, that purely human "progress" would increase goodness – that delusion has been utterly disappointed, utterly frustrated in our day. But not the Gospel! Hear our Lord's own symbolic description of the future of the world which He was about to die to redeem:

Nation shall rise against nation and kingdom against kingdom and there shall be great earthquakes in divers places, famines and pestilences upon the earth, distress of nations with perplexity, men's hearts failing them for fear and for looking after things which are coming on the earth.

That is human history considered in itself, as He focuses it, not just at the end of the world, but in long-drawn perspective. And then comes the Christian conclusion and the Christian hope: "When these things begin to come to pass, then look up and lift up your hearts *for your redemption draweth nigh.*" The Christian hope lies not in what happens within human history, in the *process* of earthly history. It lies in something from beyond history – the redemption of God. That penetrates all history, it makes human history serve its purpose at every end and turn, it judges history, but it does not *transform* human history into itself. Our hope lies not in the improvement of mankind by their own increase in knowledge and power. It lies in the action of God, redeeming – not the world – but the individual men and women in it, never *against* their wills, never *without* their own efforts, but never *by* their own wills and efforts alone.

That is why it is so good for us to turn for a while from the formidable judgements of the Lord upon the nations to the figure of Mary, the mother of fair love: a single human figure, radiant but tiny in the vast perspective of the centuries; so ordinary, so weak, and yet of such infinite significance in human history; the young girl with the *unique* vocation without whom the arm of the Lord would have been shortened, without whom the redemption of men by God could never have been wrought – even though it was God that wrought it – grimly and murderously out of His own Flesh and Blood, from *within* our real world of sin and calamity, our world as we know it.

That is her significance, that the holy Body and the Precious Blood which were to be the very ransom of men and women, the very instruments of God's redemption, were not His own. He was made man of the very substance of the Virgin Mary His mother and only by Her consent. They were drawn from Her immaculate heart, made from Her untainted Blood in her Virgin womb who said "Behold the handmaid of the Lord. Be it unto my according to thy word". The most august words that ever passed purely human lips, because she alone thereby ever freely *gave* to God the only thing not His by right – "creatureliness".

The consequence, the immediate consequence of the Annunciation, is the Visitation. Mary's greatness is twofold – not only to give humanity to Jesus but to give Jesus to humanity. Hard on the Annunciation comes the Visitation. Why did she go? Origen, in the very first Christian commentary on St Luke's gospel, says that she went to carry Jesus to sanctify John the Baptist in the womb. For that is the striking thing. Mary, for all her greatness, is not an isolated factor or agent in the plan of God. God has been at work long before Archangel Gabriel was sent to Nazareth. There are Zechariah and Elizabeth, and back behind them all the prophets and seers and priests and just men of Israel, all the dim hopes and longings of men for God back to the very morning of the world. And now the forerunner, the very climax of all these centuries of hope and preparation is in the womb of his mother, yet he is but man. He needs, he must have, sanctification, even he of whom it was said that among men born of women there hath not arisen a greater than John the Baptist – even he cannot of himself, of mere humanity, rise to the height of his vocation. He needs redemption even in the womb. You know the story, how the unborn babe leaped for joy when Mary brings Jesus, prophesying the Saviour in the darkness before dawn. Mary brings Jesus to sanctify John by His very presence. Yet outwardly Mary only goes to render a kindly service to a cousin needing help. It is her relation to Jesus which gives a profound *theological* significance to her faithful discharge of a womanly duty.

So with us. We are members of Christ. Redeemed by His Precious Blood to be sons of God, who were given Mary for their Mother from the Cross itself. We have to help each other and the world to God not only by our prayers but by our living. In our degree we have to give Jesus to humanity. It is our relation to *Jesus* which gives our ordinary faithfulness or failure its profound *theological* significance, not only for ourselves but for the world and God's plan for it. But that is true for all Christians. For us there is rather more in it than that. We look out on a world today that writhes in the agony of spirit that is the consequence of its own alienation from God – and yet does not repent, a disenchanted world which scarcely dares to think of the present and only hope without much expectation for a peace which it fears will mean a turmoil rather less tremendous than its war. Very little now of that liberal illusion that was so manifest after the last war. But even *this* world is still *God's* world. He is still at work in it. Though it looks so barren, no word from God shall be void of power. All hangs for the world upon the faithfulness of the Church to this truth. And far more hangs for the Church upon *our* faithfulness to it than upon that of most others. We are men who have seen most clearly that the world is God's, and *therefore* that men and women matter literally *infinitely* more than *any* human institutions. We have tried to act drastically and thoroughly upon that clear knowledge, to live our whole life upon it – because it is the ultimate bed-rock fact about human living. St Benedict went to his cave at Subiaco driven by just the same clear-sightedness. He lived when civilisation was collapsing, when the Church was rocking to its very foundation, riddled with heresies and rent with schism and after schism. He went to Subiaco to be a good monk, which means *to be a man wholly living to God.* And so he learned how to teach others to be good monks. There was no more to it than that. And the Benedictines saved civilisation, and so far as men may be said to save a Divine Institution, they saved the Western Church, as a by-product, a mere corollary, of being good monks. Are you and I living like that? I think it a good preparation for St Benedict's feast this week to consider Blessed Mary at her Visitation. Every action in which *I* am faithful – the little *I* – the individual man – so dear to God – every faithfulness of mine has its own eternal consequence, and also its *theological* significance for the Church and world in history, just because of my relation to Jesus. God is not only the Judge of the Nations and the Lord of History. He is the sovereign Lord and Redeemer of my individual soul, the guide of my individual life, who treasures and uses every action in it that I will give him. He is the joy and the reward, just because He is the source and end of the human being that I am.

## St Mary Magdalen

*In this sermon, preached in the morning of 22 July 1945, at the Patronal Festival of St Mary Magdalen, Paddington, London, Dix emphasizes Mary Magdalen's role as 'apostle to the apostles' above other traditions associated with her, and uses her life and witness as a reminder of the 'intimate dependence' of individual members of the Church upon one another within the Body of Christ.*

[John 20.18] "Mary Magdalen came and told the disciples that she had seen the Lord and that He had said these things to her".

The English of the Authorized Version conceals, a little, I think, the simple vividness of the Evangelist's Greek in translating this verse. You might render it literally: "Mary Magdalen came proclaiming to the disciples that . . . ". "Told the disciples" hardly reflects the solemn and exultant tone of the word St John uses for "proclaiming" here. One old translation of the Gospel into Syriac made in Palestine which very often carries over the ideas of the first Jewish-Christian disciples uses instead a very significant word: "There comes Mary Magdalen *evangelising* the disciples that she had seen the Lord". Her message on that first Easter day was in very fact the heart and core of the "good news", the first tremendous piercing flash of the explosion of the primitive Christian gospel.

All of us, of course, know very well Mary's part in the events of Easter morning. No one could ever forget the loveliness or the significance of the story, told so exquisitely by St John, of the brief dialogue in the garden at dawn, when she supposing Him to be the gardener turned at His simple question "Lady, why weepest thou, what seekest thou?" in entreaty that she may be given back a corpse; and through her tears discerns, against all human hope, the Prince of Life. "Jesus saith unto her, 'Mary'". It is the perfect recognition scene, the ultimate art of writing in its simplicity. And it is more than art; it is life! For it forces from the most casual reader the instinctive recognition of his own accord: "This is true! It must have happened like that; it could only have happened like that".

But though none of us can really fail to be aware of the part that fell to Mary Magdalen in the garden of Joseph of Arimathea – "that better part that shall not be taken from her" as long as the world shall last, while men place their dearest hopes in the fact of Easter – yet I think it is true that to most Christians this is not as a rule the first thought which comes unbidden to our minds when we hear the name of Mary Magdalen. Men think first of all of the more flamboyant, perhaps more humanly *interesting*, figure of the splendid beautiful sinner who became the broken, weeping penitent. We remember that clearly, even though the New Testament tells us singularly little personal detail about it when you come to analyse what it does tell us of her. And one sees and remembers, too, the fittingness that Mary the Penitent should have stood beside Mary Immaculate at the foot of the cross. But I think it is of these things, Mary at the feet of Jesus and of the supper at Bethany, with its picturesquely sad anointing of our Lord for burial that one thinks instinctively and first of all in connection with her, rather than of Mary Magdalen in her greatness of Easter morning, *as the Apostle to Apostles and the Evangelist to Evangelists*. Yet that is undoubtedly how St John represents her here. And I would remind you that this is the last mention of her in the New Testament. From henceforward all is silence about her in authentic history, and it is only long afterwards and in very dubious legends that the attempt is made to carry on the story. In fact, it could hardly be carried on significantly at all from such a point. That is what Mary the sinner of Magdala had become – and here the Scriptures leave her, a woman with a privilege not so superhuman as unique in its own very different way as that of the sinless Mary of Nazareth herself. That is why I have preferred to set her before you on this her feast-day in her own Church, not as what she made herself as what, in the end, she became and was made by the grace and person of Jesus, the herald to the heralds of the world's redemption. As I say, the scriptures tell us very little about her sins except the fact of them, and only a little more about her penitence, because that is chiefly her affair. The scriptures never gossip, are never sentimental and never morbid. But they do tell us every detail of that minute of her glory in the garden, because that is what God made of her, and the scriptures are the story of the mighty works of God with the children of men. And with that glory they leave her and fall silent, to speak of other mighty words of God with other sinners – Peter and Thomas and Paul and many others.

One hardly could say more in her honour on her feast-day than the Holy Spirit has put it into the pen of the Evangelist to say simply by recounting the facts of Easter morning. Yet perhaps it is as well to draw a moral, to find for ourselves a lesson to think about. There are many, but perhaps this is as useful and good a one as any for us to think about at this present time. It is this – the intimate dependence of all the members of the Body of Christ upon one another from the least to the greatest. It is not that there are not appointed offices and functions, involving special duties and responsibilities and powers in the Church. But the greatest Pope and wisest Bishop and the most learned theologian and the holiest saint must serve God from within the Body, never apart from it; and are therefore in part dependent on all the other members of the Body for the fulfilment of their own special functions. No Christian *can* live to God alone – not even the greatest. There is a continual mutual dependence, even though this does not do away with special functions and responsibilities. There is the responsibility of *ecclesia docens*, Bishops and theologians to teach and safeguard the true faith. But there is equally the continual pressure of *ecclesia discens* of the faithful laity and the pastoral clergy upon the hierarchy to do so, exercised all the time by the fact that they *believe and practise* the truth.

The Catholic Church can show us overwhelmingly imposing lists of great leaders, great saints, great scholars, great statesmen, great creative souls of all kinds, men and women of all ages. But she never puts her trust finally in any great man. No single individual, however holy or gifted, has ever been allowed to hold towards her that sort of decisive position or to exercise upon her that sort of creative influence which Luther holds for Lutheranism, Calvin for Calvinism and so on. Always for the Catholic Church even the greatest of her sons must speak "the mind of the Church", or he must be disowned. And that is something upon which the whole body of the faithful have a steady influence just by their living of the catholic life and practising of the catholic faith. It is as though the Church always unconsciously remembered that of her first twelve princes, one betrayed and one denied and ten forsook and fled, and that only one, St John, crept back in the darkness to stand beside Mary Immaculate and Mary the Penitent at the foot of the cross in the crisis of all human history; and that her first Saint in heaven was not an Apostle but a penitent thief baptized not by an Apostle but in his own blood. If ever you are tempted to forget your individual responsibility as a Catholic, the splendour and loftiness of your personal vocation as a member of the Body of Christ under the plea of being only one of the laity, remember the first Easter morning, when Peter the Rock on which the Church was to be founded and John the Eagle who would see into heaven, rushed through the dawn to see only grave-clothes in a tomb; but a woman saw and *knew* the Lord of life in a garden, and was sent to bear the very message of the gospel itself to the Apostles: "Go to my brethren and say unto them, I ascend unto my Father and your Father, and to my God and your God".

It did not do away with their apostolate. Theirs was the official commission to witness to Easter. They, and not Mary Magdalen, were, as John truly saw in a vision, the twelvefold foundation of the City of God. To Peter and not to Mary Magdalen was given the charge to feed the sheep and lambs of Christ. To Matthew and John and not to Mary Magdalen was given the inspiration to write the Gospels. Yet the fact remains that the first of all tellings of the "good news" of God, the first of all witnessings to the resurrection, they heard from the lips of Mary Magdalen.

You keep a great feast. You have a glorious patroness, not so much because much was forgiven to her who loved much, as because Mary Magdalen came and told the disciples that she had seen the Lord and that He had said these things unto her.

## Dedication Festival

*Dix preached this sermon at St Barnabas, Jericho, Oxford, for the Church's Dedication Festival on 21 October 1945. Beginning with a powerful and expansive exposition of Paul's cosmic Christological hymn of praise in Colossians Chapter 1, Dix goes on to emphasize Christ's pre-eminence in every local community, made visible by what goes on outside and inside the Church: 'being there and being obvious . . . lifting up the cross above the chimney pots, insisting on Jesus Christ as the centre of all human living'; but also, more importantly, building up the hidden life of the Christian through participation in the ongoing sacramental life of the Church.*

[Colossians 3.3, 4] "Your life is hid with Christ in God. When Christ our life shall appear, then shall ye also appear with Him in glory."

St Paul is writing to the Church of Colossae in Asia Minor, a letter of congratulation and also of tactfully conveyed reminder of the things that matter. It opens with a magnificent hymn of thanksgiving for the wonderful, unbelievable blessings and mercies of God given to mankind in the Gospel, of praise to Him "who has made us fit to be partakers of the inheritance of the saints in light; and delivered us from the power of darkness, and has transferred us into the kingdom of his dear Son; in Whom we have redemption through His Blood, even the forgiveness of sins". And then the Apostle goes on a little to insist on the all-importance of Jesus Christ, whom the Colossians were showing themselves a little inclined to take for granted. "He is the image of the invisible God" – God made manifest. "For by Him were all things made that are in heaven and that are in earth, visible and invisible, whether they be thrones or dominions or principalities or powers" – the most noble spirits and loftiest archangels all are the work of his hands, utterly dependent on Him for their very being. "He is before all things and by Him all things hold together. And He is the head of the Body, the Church, who is the beginning, the first-born from the dead" – He, the man, Christ Jesus; He, of Nazareth, the Son of Mary. It is a terrific claim to make on behalf of a criminal executed thirty years before – "that in all things He might have the pre-eminence." "For it pleased the Father that in Him" – in that Man of Flesh and Blood – "should all fullness dwell", the very plenitude of God, "that making peace by the Blood of His

Cross", by *Jesus* – by Jesus only – God would "bring all things into unity with Himself; by Him, I say, whether they be things in earth, or things in heaven". All that exists, says the Apostle, depends upon Jesus of Nazareth, not only for its coming into being, but for its continuing in being, and also for the purpose and fulfilment of its being. All this is tremendous in its sweep and scope, taking in all creation, the furthermost stars and uttermost reaches of time and hanging it all, as it were, upon Jesus of Nazareth, placing it all, the whole vast creation of God, in His human hands. But it is all very difficult to take in, to believe, to do anything about. It is all very *impersonal*.

And then suddenly St Paul turns to those actual Colossians, those individual men and women he is writing to, standing listening in the room while his letter is being read out by Tychicus. "And *you*", he says, "you that were once alienated from God and His enemies in your mind by wicked works, yet now He has reconciled *you* to God" – as well as the whole huge creation of God – *you* personally, "in the Body of His flesh through death, to present you, holy and un-blameable and unreproveable in His sight". So vast, so irresistible, so universal, yet so particular and detailed is His reconciling power that He won for Himself on Calvary, that He can make *you*, for all the unworthiness you know in yourself, to be holy and unblame-able and unreproveable, even before those burning fiery eyes of God that look down into the very depths of the most dazzling and glori-ous of the principalities and powers, the mightiest spirits round the throne of God, and discern their utter dependence and createdness. Yet even the piercing eyes of the love of God will discern no flaw, no unworthiness in you – on one condition: "if ye continue in the faith, grounded and settled, and are not shifted away from the hope of the Gospel". This is the claim of the faith – to bring men to God – to God Himself, to the abyss of all being, Infinite Joy, Perfect Truth, Beauty and Goodness in a Person, and to hold them there, for ever and ever – unreproved and unblameable – for all their littleness and created-ness – through the life and death of Jesus Christ and the redemption wrought by Him.

And the means is their own individual Baptism and Confirmation. St Paul insists that this is where their own *personal* spiritual remak-ing for God was done. It has consequences that can never be undone. Then each one of them died and rose again and ascended into heaven, even though they didn't realize it.

"If ye then be risen with Christ, seek those things", be earnest about, pay attention to, "those things which are above where Christ sitteth on the right hand of God." That is where your real life is going on, *here and now.* "Your life is hidden with Christ in God". That is the life that really matters for you – the life that is building itself up, here and now, "in Christ", in the very Being of God Himself: *your* real life, the life that will last.

We know that life in time won't last for ever. Our Lord Jesus Christ, in the scriptures, and modern scientists all assure us that the universe is running down like a clock all the time. The sun, moon and stars will cease to be. We shall remember constellations as we now remember our childhood or a house we lived in many years ago. However, the life in God will never be over. This is the stupendous consequence of redemption, of being transferred to the kingdom of His dear Son. When Christ our life shall appear, it shall be made as obvious and real to us as our earthly life is to us with all its apparatus, as real to us as the chairs we are sitting on and the bricks and mortar of these walls are to us at this minute. Then *we*, our real selves, the selves built up in Christ, "will appear", will be manifest and obvious to ourselves, "with Him in glory". That is the faith, the promise of the Gospel.

You are keeping your Dedication Festival, a time when we remind ourselves like the Colossians of the immense privilege of having "been made fit to be sharers of the inheritance of the saints in light". Those holy and generous men and women, Fr Noel[1] and the people of St Barnabas in his generation, by whose earnestness and goodness and self-sacrifice this Church was raised, they have gone on into that inheritance, the unspeakable joy and glory of God. If they are not all already in enjoyment of it, at least we may believe that their purification in Purgatory is already nearing its end. We shall pray for the souls of all benefactors and worshippers and priests at this mass. And we are to follow them, sooner or later, in ten, twenty or fifty years. So short a time. But a Dedication Festival always has in it that double aspect of the things of which St Paul speaks. There is the Church, the material building we can all see, both from outside and from inside. Outside it stands up among the houses of the Parish; dominating them, insisting just by being there and being obvious, on the fact of God, on His supreme claim on even the earthly lives of men, lifting up the cross above the chimney pots, insisting on Jesus Christ as the centre of all human living. That is the grand outstanding fact in all the history of mankind: that in all things He must have pre-eminence.

But striking as its witness is, the outside is not what matters most. That is what happens *inside*. The souls remade, built up in God, are what will last. After centuries this Church will cease to be, but the souls delivered from the power of darkness in that font; the souls transferred into the kingdom of His dear Son in confirmation; "the souls alienated from God and enemies of Him in their minds by wicked works yet now reconciled" in these confessionals; the souls presented holy and unblameable and unreproved in His sight in the body of His Flesh "through His death" in every mass – these souls will never pass away. Their life, your life in Christ, your true and endless life is going on, secretly, hiddenly, but decisively, irremovably, indestructibly, enduringly, eternally. All the time, even though it be hidden from your eyes with Christ in God, it is in the eyes of the Holy Angels, of God Himself, the realest thing that ever happens in this Parish, that shall *never* pass away. When Christ, who is our life shall appear, be revealed as the mainspring of all existence, in eternity, then shall *you* also appear – baptized, confirmed, absolved, made One with Him – redeemed, in glory.

## Note

1. Montague Henry Noel was the first vicar of St Barnabas, Jericho. The church was consecrated in 1869.

## The Eucharist – Preparation and Thanksgiving

*This passage forms the concluding part of a sermon on the Eucharist delivered as a mission address on 15 February 1951 in the United States. A common theme in Dix's writings is his emphasis on the Eucharist as an upward rather than a downward action. For Dix, the Church does not drag God's holiness down to the level of human sinfulness, but in the sacrifice of the mass sinful humanity is lifted up to God's holiness: 'It isn't we who receive Him, it's He who receives us'.*

I want to say just a few things about preparation before and thanksgiving after Holy Communion.

I believe there is a very rightful kind of anxiety among lots of good lay people about preparing worthily for their Communion. So there should be. We ought to examine our conscience. We ought to detest our sins. We ought to beg our Lord to make us fit for our Communion. But never suppose that apart from His mercy we ever could be fit.

Don't let a sense of unworthiness keep you from communicating. The dreadful thing would be if you really thought you were worthy. On the other hand if you wait until you are worthy you'll never receive Communion again. So don't let a sense of unworthiness keep you from Communion.

Prepare for your Communion. People sometimes say, "Well, how should I prepare?" Some people aren't very much helped by set forms. They read some of those admirable prayers that you get in Communicant Manuals, and you say, "Well, I see that is the kind of thing I ought to want to say, but it doesn't really come alive to me and somehow I can't really make it seem very real to me." Don't worry, quite often the best sort of Communion preparation is to say over and over again one or two simple short acts which do say the thing you want to say. "Come and reign over my life. Thy kingdom come in me. Thy will be done in me as it is in heaven." Those things said with just the sheer desire of your heart that you may be His and He may be yours – is a far better preparation than reading over admirably phrased prayers which perhaps don't mean very much to you. You don't impress our Lord with finely wrought prayers and you aren't rejected because your prayers are a bit incoherent. He looks at your heart. He looks at your desire. If you want Him, want to be His and Him to be yours, and you want to proclaim before angels and men and God Himself that Jesus' death upon the Cross was the sacrifice of the Messiah bringing man to God, you're bound to make a good Communion.

Feel whatever you may. Some people are so constituted that religious emotion comes easily to them. Some people never feel a thing. That's got nothing to do with it. Feeling is very largely a matter of psychological, temperamental makeup, very often a matter of physical health; but don't bother about whether you feel. Just want with your will to be His. Want Him to be yours. When you've done that you are ready for Communion.

And then Thanksgiving. There again people say, "I go away from the Altar and it doesn't mean a thing. I get out in the street and I forget all about it. I go home and in the evening I remember and say a prayer or two of thanksgiving, but surely that isn't the right way". I'm not sure. Our Lord did not give us the Holy Communion so that we could indulge in devotional wallowings. He gave it to us so that we could go out into life with His strength in us. Very often that is largely our conscience. But I believe that the best kind of thanksgiving, and you can manage it, is made four or five minutes after the service – to be practically silent, to be content, to be in His hand, to keep looking back to the Lord your precedent, to let Him look down into your soul and have His own way with you. You don't try and say much. Your mind will wander, bring it back but just so it will be before Him, His.

We so often think about receiving our Lord in Communion. Of course, that is one way of looking at it. But there is a much truer way, you know. We don't bring down His greatness to our littleness. We can't pull His strength down to our weakness. We don't drag down His holiness to our sinfulness. No, it's the other way about. We are taken up, lifted up, out of our littleness into His greatness, our sinfulness is swallowed up in His holiness, our weakness is poured out into His strength. It isn't we who receive Him, it's He who receives us.

What has been slowly dawning before us as we come through the Mission has been this very fact of a vast and mighty plan of God to bring man, all men, into a unity with Himself, reflecting His glory, in which every man and every woman has his or her unique place. I want to talk more about that plan tomorrow night. But there is that vast over-arching plan of God, going from Creation to the Judgement and beyond. And the centre of that plan, so to speak, the climax, the crisis, is Jesus of Nazareth, His life, death and resurrection. We do proclaim His death, not the fact that He died, not that He died on the cross, but that His death is the death of the Lord, the master of all history, and by His death He masters history and has mastered me. I proclaim that at Holy Communion.

Holy Communion is not just a private affair of my own self, it is where I take my place in that vast, sweeping plan of God for all mankind. I take my own unique place, I take it in allegiance to, in my right relationship with Jesus of Nazareth. There I enter in His offering of Himself, which is the master stroke of that plan, but there I am caught up into, I enter into of my free will, the whole plan of God for heaven and earth. That is something in which I may be very content. I want to stay a few moments after Communion just being part of the Body of Christ in His hands, living with His life, before I go out. I need to carry on that thought into that real life of which I am a little bit of a part of the world's history, real life in the making, in which God has placed me, bringing me His kingdom there. It seems to me that is a wider view of what happens to me in Holy Communion.

Indeed He does come to me, but far more truly, far more deeply, I am taken up into Him, in Him I find my place in God's kingdom.

That is why I said, when you are giving thanks, it's a good thing to spend just two or three minutes silently, as soon after the service as you can manage it, being a member of Christ, letting Him be the life of you, without much said. That is real Communion – really being made one. On the strength of that you can go on out into the world to be a member of that world.

# Part Three

# Shaping the Religious Life

# Retreat on the Holy Rule

*Dix gave this Retreat on the Holy Rule to his brothers at Nashdom towards the end of his life. Shaped and formed by the Rule of Benedict, the community went into retreat twice a year, their 'holiday with God', as Dix called it. The retreat is divided into nine addresses. The two passages included in this chapter (from the first and the eighth addresses) give a valuable insight into Dix's understanding both of the religious life and of the nature of prayer.*

## Motives of Retreat

When we come into retreat, it is always a useful thing to begin by giving ourselves a motto or central thought. Then if the addresses prove uninteresting or not to the point, or our own meditations are unfruitful, and we come into the danger of not putting out that effort of patient and deliberate attention upon God which is what a retreat requires of us, we have always a rallying-point for our own thoughts and prayers upon which we can fall back, and from which we can advance again to make our way into the presence of God. And so I suggest to you now for such a motto or central thought, St Paul's prayer for the converts in Asia Minor many of whom he had never seen – "That being rooted and grounded in love, ye may be able with all the Saints . . . to know the love of Christ which passeth knowledge, that you may be able to be filled with all the fullness of God." (Eph. 3.18–19)

That is a very bold, and even paradoxical, prayer. But at all events, it sums up pithily enough for the purpose of a Retreat, and even of the Religious Life itself. That is why we left the world – that we might know the love of Christ which passeth knowledge and so be able to be filled to every secret corner and cranny of our being with all the fullness of God – that there might be nothing in me – in my will, my thoughts, my desires, my bodily being, which was kept back for *me*, to be my own – but all – every thought, action, moment, might be *His*, freely open for Him to enter into, to make His own. And that is why I have now put aside for a few days even the normal preoccupations of that specially dedicated state, so that I many "know" more deeply, more vividly, more responsively, that love of Christ for my single individual soul, that love which is ceaselessly surrounding me, pouring in upon me, giving life to me, in a way which I do not ordinarily recognise.

That love is like the rays of the sun streaming in all the time upon the earth, preserving, stimulating, fecundating all life upon it. The earth may cover itself with clouds; still those rays pour upon it through the clouds though their source can no longer be seen. As the earth rolls on its way, part of its surface is always turning away from the direct beams. Even so the warmth of the sun and its light reflected by the moon follow it through the night. Whether in winter or summer, night or day, the beams of the sun are the sole protection of our world against the deadly cold of inter-stellar space. If they were to cease to be lavished upon it, if our world could break free from its endless circling round their source – in a very few hours this would be a *dead* world, inky dark and frozen stiff, whizzing for ever through space, without purpose or significance or even any future possibility of its own.

So it is with our souls and God. We are bound to Him, as our earth is bound to the Sun, with bonds not of our making but of His. We are drawn from His Being, we are ceaselessly dependent on Him in all ways for our life. We may sin and hide Him from us. But our clouds cannot shut out His irradiation of us.

## Prayer

I find it acutely embarrassing to speak to you of prayer, because one has nothing but commonplaces to say of one's own about it, and at first sight St Benedict is surprisingly unhelpful. He has, of course, many incidental references to it, but these take his doctrine about it for granted. And that doctrine when it is set out, rather unexpectedly late in the Rule, turns out to be surprisingly skimpy, two little Chapters, one of three sentences and one of four. And six of these sentences look like obvious platitudes, and two of those more or less repeat each other – and the seventh is the direction that corporate mental prayer *omnimo breviatur* – shall be kept quite short. Compare this with the detailed directions for the reception of guests.

Obviously this is not all the author of the Holy Rule knew about prayer, and it is disconcerting that this was all he thought it necessary to tell his monks about it. But that was the ancient way – to be detailed and explicit about ascesis and the training of the soul and will and to be very reserved indeed about prayer . . .

Cassian, quite exceptionally, has two long Conferences on "Prayer" by Abbot Isaac which are a sort of psychological, analytical treatment – very interesting indeed. He starts with the idea, common to all spiritual writers, that we *make* ourselves what we are at our prayer, by what we are at other times. If you are lax, unrecollected, curious, over-busy in your life you will be slack, distracted, impatient, unsatisfied in your prayer . . . He then goes on to define the different kinds of prayer – and here I think we begin to see daylight.

"*Oremus* – we pray when we renounce this world and promise that we will serve the Lord with all the attention of heart and mortify all worldly actions and behaviour. We pray when we promise to despise all worldly honours and earthly riches and cleave to the Lord in compunction of heart and poverty of spirit. We pray when we promise that we will always observe chastity of body and immovable patience and root out from our heart anger and sadness that worketh death." Another kind of prayer is "when moved by fervour of spirit, we are wont to pray for others, whether for our own dear ones or for the peace of the whole world" and so on. "Or when the mind remembers past blessings of God or when it looks ahead to what great things God hath prepared for them that love Him." "Often" he says "these prayers are richer when it contemplates these, and our soul is spurred on to pour out unspeakable thanksgivings to God with immense joy." Then he goes on to speak of that "fiery prayer" which men can neither understand nor describe into which men are rapt with a burning heart. He has several descriptions of this "fiery prayer", *ignata*, which is clearly an infused and contemplative prayer of a high order. But what I want to point out is that for him it is *all* just *prayer* from elementary taking and keeping your vows of stability and obedience and amendment, and living in simplicity of heart and patience and interceding, to this high supernatural union, it is all *prayer*.

It is just here that I think there is the biggest mental barrier between the mind of St Benedict and the modern Benedictine. The medieval Western Church, beginning with St Bernard, or perhaps before him, with the Cluniacs, has "psychologised" prayer, has tended to make it purely a mental activity with conscious *felt* interior reactions. And the Renaissance, coming after this, has made Prayer – as it made everything else – an "art", with a skilled technique of its own. For the older, simpler, tradition, prayer was a not an act or an art. It was a *state* – almost a "state of life" – into which a man entered and which could and should be expressed in his whole way of life. It had its traditional rhythm and pattern as any other way of life has. It had its high soaring peaks of intensity, when as Cassian puts it, "prayer reaches beyond sound of voice or movement of the tongue or any uttered word, when the mind is narrowed by no human speech . . . but all its senses gathered in one round, leaps like a sparkling fountain towards God, discovering in one brief particle of time such things as cannot easily be spoken nor can the mind traverse again when it comes back upon itself", and its normal, steady centring the whole mind and strength and will upon God. But it was the *life* that was the "prayer".

St Benedict belongs to this world and this tradition, and we are monks of the twentieth century, who inherit from the Middle Ages and the holiness of later times a method of prayer and an approach to prayer which is rather different from his. We cannot go back even if we would. And the later piety has enriched the spiritual life and clarified some of its difficulties, even if it has brought its own difficulties of increasing the danger and the desire of wanting to watch ourselves praying in our minds instead of looking at God. St Anthony of the desert once said "That monk is not yet truly praying who knows that he is praying" – so little did the return upon self enter into the old idea of prayer.

Yet I think there is still a vital lesson to be learned from the older idea that it is the *life* itself – in all its aspects, housework, study, doing accounts, writing letters, eating meals, gardening, retreats and all the rest of it – besides the strictly devotional and so to speak "ecclesiastical" aspects – which is the prayer – because it is a vowed life. Prayer in its simplest elements is the going forth of your little created human spirit from itself to meet the downrush of the uncreated Spirit of God. We do not see Him; our minds cannot conceive Him; we cannot, in this life, know Him as He is. We can and do *love* Him as He is. That is how we apprehend Him – our love grasps and lays hold on and embraces the whole God, the real God, God Himself whom our minds cannot embrace by understanding. That is prayer. But you do that, too, you know, when you go forth from self in patience under provocation for the love of God, when you go forth from self in obedience to an inconvenient bell for the love of God, when you go forth from self in self-renunciation of all kinds for the love of God – just as much as in prayer. You do it differently, it is true, less consciously perhaps and less formally but just as really.

You do it with your *life* and not entirely with your mind. But none the less you do it with your will – the likeness of God in you. And your God is a consuming fire. That is small comfort when prayer is dry and distracted and we seem to get no further and God seems never to answer. But still it is true. You can only embrace that blankness, which is God, and say "My life shall love you if you will not kindle love in my mind".

Perhaps upon this background St Benedict's two little Chapters on Prayer take on a rather different aspect. At least I have come to find it so in the last twelve or eighteen months. Those six dry and jejune sentences, as I used to think them, have begun to seem to me to express the gist of the matter. They express an *attitude* towards the fact and the goodness and the glory of God rather than an aspiration, something which has to be distilled drop by drop so to speak from our whole life, not a special direction for times of prayer. Our life does not have two sections, prayer-time and not-prayer-time. It is the *whole man* who must go to God in prayer and out of prayers – and our God is a consuming fire.

## The Prayer of the Members

*Dix gave this address as part of a Christmas retreat to the Sisters of the Church which he led from 30 December 1937–6 January 1938. In this, the eighth of thirteen addresses, Dix considers the relationship between the prayer of Jesus, the prayer of the Church, and the prayer of the individual.*

Words from the Liturgy at Mass: "As our Saviour Christ hath commanded and taught us we are bold to say 'Our Father'".

We have contemplated so far the central fact of our lives – the truth that the life of the Christian is the life not of an isolated being but of a member of Christ and of a member of a body; we are all members one of another. A Christian who is outside the Body of Christ is an impossibility; there can be no isolated Christians.

Now we come to the fact that the prayer of the Christian – and prayer is the most important effect of that life – is and must be the prayer of a member. If we want to know how to pray we must take the prayer of the Body as our pattern. Our prayer is so partial, so imperfect, so insufficient, that it cannot be acceptable. We don't go to God as "alone to the Alone". Our prayer is made holy by the fact that it is the prayer of a member, or part of a body. The prayer of the Head becomes the prayer of the members; it is the source of all prayer. The "Spirit of Jesus" is a beautiful name given to the Holy Spirit, and we have received that spirit of adoption whereby we cry "Abba Father". "The Spirit Itself beareth witness with our spirit that we are the children of GOD." Only so can we take upon our lips that word which St Paul must have learnt from the other Apostles, "Abba", the Aramaic word for "Father" which was ever on our Lord's lips. We are children at ease with our Father, we have free access to Him. Let us now look at the prayer of the Christian from three points of view, *viz*. the prayer of the Head, Jesus Christ; the prayer of the Body, the Church; and thirdly, and *only then*, the prayer of the individual members, because it is only as members that we pray.

1. **The Prayer of our Divine Lord.** Prayer is the very substance of His Life. "Lo, I come to do Thy Will" are the words applied to Him from the first moment of His coming into the world. He, the God-man, is the perfect *adorer* of his Father. As God the Word He is the expression of *all* the holiness of God, He is the canticle of praise which God perpetually sings to His own holiness. The Word is the perpetual praise which God's holiness renders to the holiness of God. As Man He is the perfect realisation of the human creature's worship. He taught His followers "always to pray and not to faint," which is something that He Himself practised always. It was human prayer, real prayer, offered by His Sacred Humanity to His Father. Our Lord's life is a Liturgy, a perfect oblation offered to the glory of the Father. His days of labour and nights of prayer are the outward expression of His worship. All through He was actively and continually perfectly united to His Father with never a moment's distraction. His was a service perfectly and completely rendered. He gathers up His life's worship and carries it to a peak of intensity in His supreme oblation of Himself on the Cross. *All* is worship all through His life, and all is summed up and directed towards Calvary and the Sacrifice of the Cross. That Sacrifice is the unique and transcendent worship of the perfect Priest and the perfect Victim. Therefore it is not merely a prayer, nor even the *greatest* prayer, it is more splendid and powerful than all others, it is ideal prayer. It *is* prayer, absolute, unique, total prayer which has taken up into itself all human prayer which has ever been and ever will be uttered, and makes them acceptable, not merely because He is God, or the holiest of men, but because He is *by nature* the only link, the Divinely-appointed link between God

and man. He is the Priest of the race of men, and the *only* way to God. "I am *the* Way. No man cometh to the Father but by Me." We are accepted *in* the Beloved. All blind humble prayers offered to the Unknown God find their voice in Him before the Throne of God. Because His prayer is uniquely perfect, the only prayer accepted by God, the only perpetually efficacious prayer, "He ever liveth to make intercession for us," "in earth as in heaven". The Lamb "as It had been slain" was seen by St John in his vision of heaven. The prayer of Jesus, the holocaust of Jesus, is perpetuated not only in heaven but also in the world in the Holy Mass. Its frequency and commonness must never blind us to that. Through all lands and all centuries it goes on; it is renewed without ceasing and there is never a moment when the Holy Mass is not being said somewhere. That unique and wholly efficacious Prayer has many jewels but none that shines with the glory of the Mass. That total and sufficient Prayer, which is the strength and significance of *all* prayer, is continued on earth in the Mass. In that Prayer, the Mass, is offered not only the prayer of the Head, but also the prayer of the members. It is offered not only *by the Head* but also *by the members*. The prayer of the Head takes up into itself the sacrifice of the members. The Sacrifice of the Head takes up into itself the sacrifice of the members. That Prayer which is unique and sufficient in itself has its extension in the prayer of the Church. The Church is a Body and Soul, so she has a public and an invisible life. Thus there is its public extension in the Liturgy, and its private and interior extension in Christian devotion. The first is the prayer of the Body as a whole, and the second is the prayer of the members still praying of course *as members*. The prayer of the Church is the extension of the prayer of the Holy Mass.

**2. The Divine Office.** So we come to consider the Divine Office as the extension of the Mass. The Divine Office is the special glory and duty of us Religious. It is not something which a person makes up for herself. Do not let us underestimate the value of private prayer, but we must remember that private prayer has no value at all comparable to the value of the Divine Office. It is the prayer of the Body of Christ. The Mass is the heart of our worship. It is the Mass that gives our worship its value. It is as if the Sacrifice moves on from Church to Church, but each local Church remains grouped around its own Altar, and the prayer of the Head and the members together continues. It is a wonderful thought. I never cease to love the idea of Religious Communities grouped around the Blessed Sacrament of the Altar continuing, in the Divine Office, that worship which is rendered in the Mass. That shows what the Divine Office really is – the prayer of the members offered *through* the Head. "All glory be to GOD in the Church through Jesus Christ." He is the soul of all worship. We must always remember when we have to say the Office far away from Choir, that because we are members of our Society our recitation of the Divine Office is the prayer, not of one person having to hurry through the Office in some unworthy corner perhaps, but of the Body. It is well to make it obvious in our Choir that it is to the Tabernacle that we pour the Office. So the Head and the members are not separated. "All glory to God in the Church by Jesus Christ" – *in* the Church, not just in my heart. *By* Jesus Christ, for He is the soul of it. It is at the Divine Office we see its magnificence. Wherever it is said we see its variety, its adaptability, its pliability, its poetry, beauty, antiquity. The same psalms are used constantly yet by different antiphons we get a different spirit at the varying seasons. But we are not only thinking of its beauty and antiquity – though there is a thrill in the fact that we are using hymns in the Hours which were used by St Augustine of Canterbury. Nor are we even only thinking of the fact that every generation has added of its very best in the Divine Office, nor that so much of its text has the Holy Spirit as its Author – and no other prayer has that – but *the* fact that makes the Liturgy so glorious is that in it the Church is joining her holiness, which is the holiness of her Spouse, to the perfect holiness of God the Word as He worships His Father. That is what the Church sets upon my sinful lips. No wonder that before beginning the Office we pray, "O Lord, open Thou my lips." The Divine Office is the context of the Mass in which God sets that jewel. The glory of the Office is that it is not *my* prayer, however well I may say it, but that it is the Bride joining her voice with that of her Spouse. It can blend with the celestial voices of Angels and not sound harsh because it is His voice *in* His Mystical Body. So in the Office let us never forget that we are prolonging the grandeur of the Mass. It is Vocal Prayer and that is why wherever we say it we should form it with the lips that it may be a kind of voice. Lack of fervour on my part in saying the Office when perhaps I am very tired or even bad-tempered does not affect the *Office*. On such days I still can and must and do say my Office because it is not mine, but because it is the prayer of the *Head and the members*. I pray in the name of the Church. I say what the Church gives me to say, neither more nor less. What is essential is to pray in the Name of Christ.

Never imagine from what I have said that I encourage a pharisaical saying of the Office; it is of course best to say it with devotion, but whether that is there or not it must be said. The foot fulfils the function of the body though it may have pins and needles and not want to walk, but all the same the body is carried forward by it. The Office does indeed suggest devotion as no other devotion can, but it does not always express what *I* feel at the moment. *I* may be cast down over something and the Church may at that moment set words of joy on my lips, and another day when I have not had such a bad time she may give me the words of the *Miserere* to say. What I am expressing in the Office is the praise, the contrition, the self-immolation of all the members of Christ, mourning for those who are being repentant and rejoicing for those who are praising without being conscious of what they are doing. It expresses joy, repentance, worship, praise, thankfulness, oblation, self-immolation. All those unconscious followings of Christ in human life it makes conscious. Because we are members one of another we can, though those other members may never know, seize upon all those things and turn them into the glory of God. So the Divine Office is the function of Religious sanctifying the life of the Body. All the patience, energy and suffering of those Christians who don't realise can be made conscious and sanctified in the saying of the Office. It is as though we made the sign of the Cross over everyone's daily bread. It is our function as Religious in the Body. It is for this reason that the Church drives us back to Choir so constantly when perhaps we feel that we have had enough of it. Remember it is other people's lives that we are to sanctify when we say the Divine Office and pronounce the Prayer of the Head and the members.

**3. Private Prayer.** That also is an extension of the Mass. The Mass has two sides to it; the exterior rite which we see and hear, and the interior mystery which only faith can understand. In the Liturgy we have the exterior prayer of the Body, and in private devotion the interior mystery. Our Lord in the Mass offers the supreme worship to His Father, and His gift of Himself to His members is perpetually renewed. It is a most touching thing that what He does is incomplete, for without man that Sacrifice is incomplete until He has given Himself to men as well as to God. There can be no Mass without at least *one* communicant, that is why every Priest *must* make his Communion at every Mass he says. What an amazing thing it is that our Lord's worship of the Father should be incomplete without the members.

The *Head needs* the members. All Christians must communicate at least once a year. A Christian must communicate at every Mass. We receive Him in order that He may live to God in us. That is, the prayer of all communicants is the prayer of our Lord in them. It is as though the Church took the worshipping Christ and placed Him within each of her members that there He can continue His prayer. In former times the Priest placed the Host in the mouth of the communicant with the words, "The Body of Christ", and the communicant answered "Amen". It is a pity that that custom has disappeared for it was saying "Amen" or "So be it" to the prayer of Christ. "He ever liveth to make intercession" not only in heaven and on the Altar, but also in those to whom He comes. All we have to do is to desire what He desires. All our blind prayers are supplemented, fulfilled, perfected in Christ Who *is* our prayer, Who is perfect Prayer. From our dumbness goes up all the unspeakable and Catholic prayer of the Sacred Heart for all the human race that He came to save, for all His Holy Church, for all His Saints, those of earth and Purgatory and Heaven, for all sinners, for those who know Him not, for those who despise and persecute Him, for the lonely, the neglected, the suffering, it goes up from us. It doesn't matter if we don't realise it. All we have to do is to desire what *He* desires. The Father sees *Him* in us, and us in Him. He hears the voice of the Head in the members and the voice of all the members in the Body. When the Sacramental Presence has passed we do not lose it unless we are in unrepented mortal sin, for it prolongs itself in every word of prayer we utter. Look, then, at Christian prayer and realise how it is taken up into His prayer, like a great concert of prayer. However feeble, squeaking and flat many of the notes may be they are taken up into His. If we played them alone they would be valueless, but our notes are taken up into His prayer and there they miraculously find their harmonious place. My poor prayer, if I put my best into it, is taken up into the prayer of the Body and the Head, which is the prayer of the perfect Adorer of the Father. When we say Office in Choir no *one* person has said that Office. Before God that Office has gone up as the prayer of the Body; it is a corporate thing and is a parable of all *Christian* prayer. "As our Saviour Christ hath commanded and taught us we are bold to say" – yes, bold because He taught us – "Our Father".

## Silence in Heaven: On Contemplation and Action

*In this sermon, preached at Nashdom on 30 September 1945, the day after Michaelmas, Dix compares the calling of the angels to simultaneous contemplation and activity with that of the Religious, for whom contemplation is the source of their daily activity. Dix himself was probably absent from the monastery more often than many of his brothers, whether travelling abroad, preaching, teaching, or involving himself in ecclesiastical politics and debate. When, at the end of the sermon, he refers to the monk's inability to 'renounce the Church' and 'the grinding tension between contemplation and activity', he is surely speaking from the context of an inner conflict of which he had first-hand experience and with which he often wrestled.*

[Rev. 8.4, 5] And the smoke of the incense, which came with the prayers of the Saints, ascended up before God out of the angel's hand. And the angel took the censer, and filled it with fire of the altar, and cast it upon the earth: and there were voices, and thunderings, and lightnings, and an earthquake.

The Apocalypse is describing the worship of heaven after the sealing of the 144,000 servants of God and the significant statement that "there was silence in heaven about the space of half an hour". The silence of rapt, intense, utter contemplation succeeds for the redeemed to the world-wide bustle and business of the gathering of "the great multitude that no man can number, of all nations, and kindreds and people and tongues before the throne of God", and their first triumphant earth-shaking shout of deliverance: "Salvation to our God that sitteth upon the throne and unto the Lamb". God, who is illimitable joy, gives Himself in a torrent of goodness and of joy in that goodness to each one of His lovers, and their souls are satiated. God *is* Joy, His own Joy; it is bliss unspeakable to Him to be Himself in the profoundest depths of His own perfect Being. And now as our Lord promised, "His joy remains in them and their joy is full". And for very shock of that joy in its Divine fullness, the redeemed are silent. To be in God and with God and for God – simply *to be* thus in His beatitude – takes the full exercise of their new redeemed being – and they are silent, almost drowned in love and joy. But the majestic worship of the Angels and the Heavenly Elders with its prostrations and its pealing trumpets sounding from time to time with the sweeping melody of the choir and the symbolic ceremonial of the golden altar before the throne of God, continues to swell, apparently simultaneously with the silence, before the eyes of the sealed. It is the perfect expression of the difference between Angelic and human contemplation and service of God. And then abruptly comes this apparently irrelevant incident I have taken for my text: "And the Angel took the censer and filled it with the fire of the heavenly altar and cast it upon the earth", or "into the earth". And suddenly we are back in this world again, with its wars and disasters, its wrath and its sin and its struggle and its apparent chaos of good and evil, with the dreadful judgements of God sweeping over the nations and the triumphant joy of heaven apparently very far away as the trumpets sound for the wrath of God.

We have been keeping the feast of the Holy Angels, and perhaps feeling a little holy envy of those who even while "they serve and defend us on earth" and indulge in all manner of activity in the service of God, as our Lord said "do always behold the face of my Father who is in heaven". It is, of course, true that there is a great difference between the natures of men and Angels. Those pure Spirits do all of them, each in their own degree, behold the very Being of God, which is for them as for us the very source of all beatitude and all good. There is no other. Some Angels see it more penetratingly, see into it more deeply, than others. These are the Cherubim and Seraphim and the higher orders of the traditional hierarchy, and it gives them the opportunity to give charity one to another, by expressing what more of God they can know to their fellows who cannot pierce so far into that fiery abyss of all Being in ways that their fellows can apprehend. But all Angels, just because they are pure Spirits, by nature and by right do perpetually see the very essence of God, the face of God, perpetually. That unveiled open vision of all perfection – of goodness without flaw and without alloy, of truth without shadow or error or question, of beauty beyond all wearying is in itself all-absorbing for any created being. For outside it, or apart from it, beyond it, there can be no desire for any creature, no love, no seeking – for there is no *good* apart from Him. And it is good or what seems good to them that all beings seek and desire. For Angels and men alike, even for the Divine humanity of our Lord himself, there is no other source of good, no other end, no other ultimate purpose of being or desire, there can be none – beside Him Who is the unchangeable, boundless Good, in Whom all Good or truth or beauty that is found fragmentarily and reflectedly in creatures has its source and super-abundant cause. And that Divine essence every holy Angel knows and apprehends directly and continually for Himself, by nature and by right, and that is His everlasting beatitude, so that however urgent be his mission from God to creatures, never for one instant does Angelic activity detract from Angelic contemplation and rapture. Even in that unimaginable pre-cosmic conflict "Michael and his angels fought with the dragon and his angels and there was war in heaven", the Angels' contemplation of God never flinched. St Michael's name and war-cry "Who is like God?" remained always a question to which from the very depths of his being the Archangel returned always the same answer out of an unwavering knowledge.

It is not so with men, who are not pure spirits. We can never know the fiery testing of that single angelic temptation which in the first moment of their being shot through the armies of heaven – whether they would tread everlastingly towards this dazzling abyss of sheer goodness for its own sake, apart from and beyond themselves, or else for ever shut themselves up inwards, towards the excellence of their own beings, created so glorious and lovely by God. Their answer to that one trial fixed their destiny for ever, just because the Angels dwell in eternity, which knows no before or after. There are no second chances in eternity because no succession. We cannot know the shaking force of their temptation, just because we have not this clear vision. We men live by the *stillulae temporem*, half angel and half beast, we do tread like them always towards God or towards ourselves, but we do it as we do everything in the conditions of space and time, step by step, little by little, *measurably*. And we do not bend either to God or to ourselves with the fierce irrecoverableness of eternal beings, but reversibly, so long as we dwell in time.

We can never know the Essence of God, as we do not see Him as He is *at all* in this life. We can never have that vision while we live. We can never apprehend and lay hold on God as He is by direct knowledge at all in this world; we can apprehend truly as He is *by love*, by blind love, and only so. But just because direct vision is lacking, we can become and do become distracted from our end – God, Himself, the vision of God, who is the life of man, by the vision of creatures. The coloured surface of existence always before our eyes takes a lot of piercing. It is perpetually closing in again in front of us and we lose sight of the *reality* of existence behind it.

Our predecessors, the first monks of the Egyptian desert, were very well aware of this. They went out into the deserts just for this, for the vision of God, in a sort of passion of renunciation, not just of their own desires but of the world itself and all temporal living. They sought the desert not only for its solitude, but for its harshness, monotony and uninterestingness. Abbot Paphnutius in Cassian speaks of the "most necessary threefold renunciation" of the monk. "The first is that by which we physically put aside with contempt all the riches of the world and its possibilities". "The second is that by which we reject the good customs and the faults of all the old devices of the mind and of the flesh". "The third is that by which we withdraw our mind from all present and visible things, and contemplate only the things that shall be and long after the things that are invisible". It is very sweeping. But Cassian's *Collations* is St Benedict's book of predilection to which he sends us again and again as "the example for well-living and obedient monks and the instrument of virtues". And the desert Fathers lived what they taught. They thought of the monastic life as "the Angelic life" finding its spring and source all the time in the Contemplation of God. In their devouring thirst for God, in the terrible intensity of their concentration on him alone, they literally did seek "to renounce the world".

Monasticism which has lost its hold on that abiding principle of theirs, the principle of the absolute primacy of contemplation, is salt that has lots its saltiness. But just because men are not Angels, the Fathers of the Desert found that "the Angelic life" was not possible for men in all its full logical development. There was much heartbreakingly heroic sanctity in the desert, but there was much extravagance also and many heart-breaking failures. St Arsenius found himself distracted from his prayers by the wind rustling the dried reeds of the desert. It is the last illusion, that solitude is peace. And with their strong common sense, the Desert Fathers accepted the fact. And so the compromise of the coenobitic life – with the old distractions of *relationships* to other men, one's fellow monks, and the "strong custom of the world" in human living. And the monk found that, most distracting of all, though he could renounce the world, he could not renounce the Church, and her needs must be as paramount with him as with other Christians. It was Anthony, the father of all monks, the Abraham of monasticism, it was Anthony, the very prince of solitaries, who declared that "life and death are in the hands of our neighbour".

And so down the ages: Basil in Cappadocia, Gregory I, Gregory VII, Damian, Augustine, Dunstan, Willibrord, Boniface, Henry of Uppsala, Columba, Cuthbert, Aidan, Bernard, even Bruno. The Church has laid hands on them all.

When we feel that grinding tension between contemplation and activity, it is nothing new. It is a part of our condition as men not Angels, but men who would be monks. I suppose the danger would come if we did not feel it. *Some* activity from mere organisation of common life, we cannot avoid it. If we felt no tension at all, it would mean no contemplation, no urgent pressing towards beauty and truth and the goodness of God – for the sake of His own loveliness alone, no answering of our love to the uncreated Love by the going forth of our whole little being rushing to meet the everlasting absolute Being of God, poured out overwhelmingly upon us His creatures. For that is contemplation, and that has the primacy in our whole living of our life. We have to remember all the time that others love God, know God, trust God, serve God as well as we, but it is ours to *cleave* to Him inseparably.

Yet when His will is shown us, by Superiors, by the needs of the Church, by circumstances, then we must turn to activities because that is His Will. We shall feel the tension painfully at times because we are not Angels. For men activity does impede contemplation. Whether they are *monastic* activities still will depend, can only depend, on the quality of our own monastic life – the depth and reality of recollection, the perfection of our charity and brotherly courtesy and willing service to one another, the sincerity and simplicity of our obedience to our Abbot, the zeal of our observance of our Rule, just because that is our ordained road to God himself. We are not a collection of individuals, but a whole. Something of the Community's life goes into every activity, even of individuals: a priest hearing the confession of nuns, or preaching a sermon in a Parish Church, a lay brother sweeping a passage or getting ready a meal for a guest. If the Community's life be truly *monastic*, its works will spring directly from its contemplation. Then truly the Angel will have taken the censer and filled it with the fire of the altar and cast it upon the earth.

## Discerning a Vocation

*This letter is one of many written by Dix to Marcus Stephens, a novice in the Society of the Sacred Mission. The correspondence between them reveals an affectionate relationship which, in this letter, allows Dix to write a strongly worded response to a request*

*for help in discerning the nature of his friend's vocation – whether
he is being called to the religious life, to ordination, or to both; and,
if to the religious life, then to which community. As with his Eucharistic theology, Dix understands sacrifice to be at the heart of vocation: 'Give, give, give – that is what you have to do – to God, to your
brethren, to the Church, to the world – never to yourself.' Stephens
was later professed in the Society of the Sacred Mission, but subsequently left his community to marry and moved to Beirut.*

10 June 1936

My very dear Marcus

Thank you very much for your long (and, I may add, very perverse)
letter. I am quite sure you *must* have a Religious Vocation. You show
exactly that a) strength of mind about tackling things the *wrong* way,
b) ingenuity in finding good reasons for doing so, c) obstinate refusal
to go with confidence to your divinely-given guide, which distin-
guishes all the good novices I have ever known about three-quarters
of the way through their novitiate. This sounds cross and sarcastic on
my part. It isn't in the least, but the most sober truth.

I have read with great care and attention all you have to say. Now
*listen* and *pay attention*. You are *all* wrong in your attitude. What
God demands of you is *not* the sacrifice of your intellect. It is the
sacrifice of *your own will* continuously. Self is very prominent in the
very centre of your circle. And God ought to be, with self at the very
circumference. As thus: "Within the last three months this priestly
pastoral vocation has tended to take a more prominent place *with
me*, perhaps outweighs in *my own consciousness* the sense of call
to the Religious Life . . . *I* can still imagine *myself* called to be a lay
religious . . . " etc. etc. for two pages. I know you have to face the
question of vocation which involves some self-analysis. But you are
Jesuitising. There is not one word in *all* of it about the will of God
apart from your own subjective reactions to it. As St Anthony of
the desert told his monks: "That monk is not yet truly praying who
*knows* that he is praying". A hard saying, but true. *Leave* the question
of God's will *for you* for the time being altogether. In your mental
prayer simply get down to the majesty and unspeakable "loveliness"
of God as He eternally is and would be if He had never called you
into being. Go through the Divine Perfections, and adore the Divine
uncompounded simplicity of his being. "God *only*" is the "portion"
not only of the religious but the cleric. Whichever you are to be that

must suffice for you. Don't imagine yourself as anything. You have no right to. You *cannot* plan your future. God alone is the dispenser of that. All you have to do is to do the will of God *now* – for this day. "Sufficient unto the day is the evil thereof", is a fundamental rule of the Religious Life. Make your own the prayers of St François de Sales: 'Yes, heavenly Father, I accept everything. Yes and always yes". Sister Jane Frances told her nuns in after years that this prayer frequently repeated, *without* even *interior acquiescence*, suffices to bring a soul into a complete conformity with the Divine intention for it. And I have no doubt she spoke from experience. Leave the whole question of your future, vocation, desires, etc. completely to God. Every time the question recurs simply say: "This I leave entirely to you. I accept it from you. Give me only the knowledge of your will. I accept it all from you and for your glory, and my confusion. "Da quod jubes et jube quod vis" as St Augustine put it. "Seek peace and ensue it".

I don't like the way you speak of your Institution. You are not fair to it as I have seen it. I admit you know it and I don't, but it is not fitting that you should doubt its character as a Religious Institute *when you are not yourself making proper use of your novice-master* and admit that fact. That is fundamentally unreligious conduct and unfits you to judge the Religious Life at all.

The two alternative solutions you suggest are not solutions.

a) Priest-oblates are not religious, not being in vows of any kind. They share the life of religious to some extent and as such may wear a distinctive habit. But as I told you at Kelham I *am* a secular priest. If I were to die tonight, unless I were professed on my deathbed, Canon Law requires that I be buried in the cemetery of the local parish church by the parish priest and not by my community in our cemetery. If I thought an "oblate" was a possible way of fulfilling a religious vocation I should not be entering the Novitiate with all its attendant tiresomeness (in September). I have longed for it for years, but till my insides took their recent turn for the better it was out of the question. But an oblate is *not* a religious.

b) The priests in the Diocese of Accra are secular priests like any other diocesan clergy. The very fact that you *can* make imaginary distinctions of this kind is a proof that you are seeing this all wrong.

I know all this sounds very fierce, but it isn't meant so. You *must* face the fact that the whole question lies in the sacrifice and surrender of your *whole will* to God and nothing else. All your arguments for dragging in dogmatic questions are merely breaking this. I am sending you back your own letter so that you may read it through again and see how really *full* of *self-will* it is. Give, give, give – that is what you have to do – to God, to your brethren, to the Church, to the world – never to yourself. Once you have got hold of that I believe you will find that the deeper insight into the truths of our holy religion which God has given you is something for you to share (to give) with your brethren, not something you are to keep to yourself and hug to yourself as you are at present planning to do if you get professed. Of course, if as a junior professed you begin to lay down the law no doubt you will merely obscure those truths from everybody else. But if you regard them as a treasure God has given you *for* others, if you live them and illustrate them by your life, others will take them from you with avidity. Every soul of good will will want them just because they have made you more like God. It is the difference between the "bitter zeal" and the "good". That is the only way. (I know I am a poor example in this. Do what I say, not what I do.)

Now don't say I have gone and got impatient and rude. You may – with permission – write to me as often as ever you like, or have need, and I have the Abbot's permission to answer as often as you write. And I will do it with real gladness and such speed as I may. I have written what I have today after reflection and reading every paragraph through after I wrote it. And I shall read it all through again and think again and pray again before I send it. It comes with a very real affection and with a very heartfelt sympathy for your difficulties. But we have had many who come here for the Roman rite and all sorts of other things. (This is one of the penalties we have to pay.) Unless they can be made to see that we come here as St Benedict puts it "truly seeking God" and *nothing else*, it always ends in departure, and sometimes very sad and scandalous departure. (We have got wiser nowadays and eliminate them quickly.) That is the one and only thing that matters – NOT the *things* of God. (Ittai and Zadok!) When I said "say *your* prayers, not Cranmer's" I meant "see to it that *you* are praying – even through Cranmer's compilation – not merely criticising him." I said before, you have to make your decision on top of a very high mountain – a stern and barren place, very cold and uncomfortable. But the air is very pure and very bracing. In that atmosphere you *can* be moved *solely by Grace* and not by anything less. And it takes *all* that to make the answer, "Thou shalt worship the Lord thy God and Him only shalt thou serve" – and *mean it. That* is austerity (not having no breakfast!). And you haven't faced it yet. You are still floundering about in a warm and muggy fog half way up. Now, do scramble up a bit! And the first step is to trust God in your superiors, just because they are the superiors God has given you, not because you feel any human attraction or confidence for them. You have not the least right to say that I have helped you "in a way your novice-master couldn't do". I have already explained to you the theological reasons why that is impossible. Do get to him.

Yesterday I sustained a visit from two Roman O.S.B.'s (English). We are forming a joint committee of Roman Catholics, Orthodox and Anglicans to coordinate the Church Unity Octave literature in our three 'branches'. Perhaps the most remarkable thing that has happened is that the Trappists of Notre Dame des Dombes and the original Visitation Convent at Annecy have formed with me a "union of participation in each other's prayers and good works" for unity. We are all to say Terce for each other every day, for our common increase in the spirit of unity and growth in the religious spirit, and to pray for each other's dead. We are all hoping to bring in an Orthodox monastery. There is a proposal that I should go to Lyons next year (January) to speak at a meeting under the Presidency of the Cardinal Archbishop – but we have asked that they get Hinsley's agreement first. We don't want any uproar afterwards. But if I go into the Novitiate it will have to wait till 1938, and I think it would be better so. I feel we are rushing things a little. These are not yet steps to a solution – but they are all part of the change of atmosphere.

Your Father Director is coming to us for a day or two at the end of the month. I *am* delighted. I must cease. I have a big post. Don't fret over what I have written. Everyone has these growing pains. God only is what matters.

Ever yours affectionately *in Dño*

Gregory O.S.B.

*Part Four*

# Shaping the Church's Ministry

# The Mystical Body

*'The Revealing Church', published in 1930, was the first of many articles Dix wrote for the Nashdom journal* Laudate. *It is clear from this, as from many of his other writings, that the Pauline image of the Church as the Body of Christ is central to his ecclesiology. Here he explores what it means to talk of the Church as a mystical body.*

The authority of the Holy Church is, or should be, a spiritual authority, and not a kingdom of this world. One of the things we mean by this is that the Church is, as it were, an ambassador of eternity, who sojourns in time only to serve the interests of eternity and its exiled citizens. As such it is her claim that she alone has the effective will, the authorization and the certain power, to repatriate those exiles. The authority which such an organ of eternity will exercise must be absolute, *once it is admitted*, just because it does not act in its own name. The faith and obedience which she claims, though they are to be exercised in time, find their motive in eternity. The only alternative to submission, if we can admit that she is what she says she is, must be permanent exile. We may dispute and examine her credentials, but once their genuineness is vindicated, she must be acknowledged the only accredited channel of communication with what she represents; there can be no appeal against her till she has brought us home.

No single metaphor or simile will ever adequately describe the Catholic Church, either for her children or her enemies. St Paul of all the writers of Holy Scripture has piled up the largest number, and perhaps his favourite is that of the organism, the mystical body of Christ, that grows to the perfect stature of the whole, Head and members together, living with the same life, suffering with the same suffering, healthy with the same health. One who had heard on the Damascus road, "Saul, Saul, why persecutest thou *Me*?" (and not "My servants" or even "My members") might well understand. "The whole Christ", says St Augustine, "is the Head and the members." "He (the Father) hath given Him to be head over all things to the Church," cries St Paul, "which is His body, the *fullness* of Him that filleth all in all." We do not always remember in the Anglican Church that the "mystical body of Christ" does not mean "the *unreal* body".

"Mystical" is opposed to "Physical" not to "Real". The Physical Body, born of Mary at Bethlehem, is no more subject to growth or suffering or anything we mean by health. The equally real mystical body was born on Calvary of water and of blood, and it is by the life of that mystical body that Christian life exists in every Christian soul at this moment. That surely is real enough, even if it be mystical.

But all these descriptions really centre upon a single conception – that the Church is the depository of a final and complete self-revelation of God to humanity, which revelation contains within itself the means whereby itself and its consequences may become available for individual men and women. It is of the essence of the idea of "revelation" that it should impart certain knowledge of facts, which could not be discovered by the use of our natural reasoning faculties alone; or which, if their possibility might be deduced from speculation, their truth and actuality must remain for ever in doubt. Since "revealed" facts are thus by nature for ever beyond the certain apprehension of unaided reason, they must also be for ever beyond its unaided verification. Reason will come after, to analyse, to articulate, it may be to control and buttress; but the acceptance of a "revelation", once the giving of it is admitted, is necessarily a pre-rational act – the act of Faith.

(RC 26–7)

## Called by the Church

*In this passage from 'The Idea of "the Church" in the Primitive Liturgies', published in 1937, Dix describes how, within his Pauline ecclesiology, the calling of the Church is primary in the discernment of vocation.*

Only when we have clearly grasped the conception of the Church as a whole as the corporate priest of a divinely ordained worship, can we rightly grasp the position of the primitive Christian hierarchy. For it is a true hierarchy, its members distinguished from the laity and from one another not only by office or function, but by differences of 'order', *i.e.* of sacramental power. Yet the hierarchy is not *over* the Church, but *in* the Church. It is indeed the product of the Church, though not its creature. Bishop, presbyter, or deacon, every member of the hierarchy must be the nominee of a genuine *election* by the whole Church. This is as necessary for the lawful exercise of the sacramental power of orders as the imposition of episcopal hands. And the Pope himself cannot ordain the man of his own choice to the presbyterate without the election of the people; if they are unwilling he must plead and argue until they will consent. (Eusebius, *Ecclesiastical History*, 6.43.17) It might indeed have been said by the Church as she presented the man of her choice for ordination, 'Thine own of Thine own do we offer unto Thee,' as the later liturgies say of the Eucharistic oblation of the Church. The only factor which does not seem to have been taken into account was the man's own inner consciousness of vocation. The early Church thrust Holy Orders on many who were most sincerely reluctant to receive them, and refused many who were strongly conscious of their own call to the episcopate. It was the Church's oblation of the man for the bishop's prayer that mattered, and having offered him with her prayer she received him back as she received back the Eucharist, her own still but now taken up into the High-priesthood of Christ, that by his ministry she might receive afresh something of her own character as the Body of Christ, and the gifts of unity and the Spirit and 'the confirmation in faith and truth'.

It is hard for us whose clergy are largely the appointment of irresponsible nominators – bishops by politicians, incumbents by patrons, assistant clergy by incumbents – to realise how greatly this choice of clergy by the whole Church, taken in conjunction with the 'charismatic' (in the true sense) rather than the 'official' notion then held of the Sacrament of Holy Orders, intensified the idea of the 'spirit-bearing' Body of Christ as in itself *priestly*. It was not that the clergy were viewed in an unsacerdotal way. There was the clearest insistence on their exclusive sacramental functions. (*E.g. Apostolic Tradition*, 26.12) But they were members *of* the Church – doubtless its 'honourable members', but members only like the laity, in fact as well as in theory, set apart by the whole Body to perform its 'liturgies' and endowed by God at the Church's prayer with the power to perform them in the Body. They had their inalienable prerogatives in the administration of the sacraments, not as a sacerdotal caste, but as members of the Body. No layman could usurp those prerogatives, simply because they were ultimately the *Church's* prerogatives, and the layman had not been empowered by the Church's choice and prayer to fulfil them.[A]

(*ICPL* 130–1)

Note

A. It is to be noted that down to the fourth century the Church rejected the very *possibility* of valid orders outside the Catholic Church, because outside the Catholic Church the Holy Ghost does not operate. It is when orders begin to be conceived of as something personal to the *man*, and not as something pertaining to the Body of Christ, that difficulties begin to multiply.

## Ministry in the Early Church

*This passage, taken from the conclusion of Dix's essay, 'The Ministry in the Early Church', was published in 1946 in a collection of essays entitled* The Apostolic Ministry: Essays on the History and Doctrine of the Episcopacy, *edited by Kenneth Kirk, Bishop of Oxford. In this concluding section, Dix argues that, in the early Church, 'episkopos' was not the title of an 'order' but rather the description of anyone who fulfilled 'episkope' within a local congregation. In relating his historical survey to difficulties facing the Church of his own day (the proposed union of episcopal and non-episcopal churches in the Church of South India, as well as the desire, on the part of some, for reunion with Rome), Dix claims that it is not its history but its apostolicity which makes episcopacy the optimum and essential system of Church Order.*

If an essay such as this is not to be a mere excursion into archaeology, it must be capable of some practical application to our own contemporary problems. To me personally the value of Christian historical study seems often to arise less from its furnishing immutable, and therefore perhaps dangerously cramping, precedents from the past, than from its power to illuminate the origins and therefore the real nature and terms of present questions. There are limits to the authority of precedents, because history never repeats itself with exactitude. It is true that all history, both secular and religious – and not least the history of the twenty-five years since Versailles in both departments – abounds in demonstrations that it is not only foolish but fatal to pretend to solve the difficulties of the present without a clear understanding of their causes in the past. But it is no less true that present difficulties always contain some novel elements which the practical statesman may rightly emphasise, and with which the rigid traditionalist cannot deal adequately by the appeal to precedent alone. If the first step to a solution lies in a right historical understanding, the second lies in a clear discrimination between past and present. Both are duties of the historian, and the second is only a little less pressing than the first. It is unfortunate that it should have been somewhat neglected in much of the modern discussion of the ancient evidence on the ministry . . .

The modern attempt to reunite Protestant and Catholic ministries does in a sense reopen questions first posed in the sixteenth century. But it is one considerable difference between the periods of disruption and attempted reunion that we are now all much better equipped to handle the appeal to history. Yet it must be admitted that its modern results have so far proved disappointing in the extreme. As Streeter once remarked, modern Episcopalians have found the primitive Church Order to be Episcopalianism, Presbyterians Presbyterianism, and Independents Independency. 'But while each party to the dispute has been able to make out a case for his own view, he has never succeeded in demolishing the case of his opponent.' Yet Streeter's rather cynical diagnosis of the cause of this – that each has found only what he hoped to find – is by no means the whole truth; and there is no need whatever to accept his conclusion that the primitive Church had no discoverable principles of Church Order, but was indifferently Episcopalian, Presbyterian, or Independent in different Churches as suited the local tastes and circumstances. On the contrary, this conclusion only expresses the judgement of an enthusiastic member of the Lausanne Conference finding the primitive Church to have been Lausanne – because he hoped to do so.

No doubt we all have a natural tendency to defend the particular forms which we happen to have inherited from the divisions of the sixteenth century. But it is vastly improbable on the face of it that the embodiment of Christian ideas in the pre-Nicene period would be much like any of these modern systems, because it is most unlikely that the revolution in the Christian situation under Constantine, followed by the immense catastrophe of the break-up of the antique civilisation, followed by the chaos of seven long barbarian centuries, followed by the profound rethinking of Christian ideas in a new and specifically Western idiom during the Middle Ages and the agitations of the sixteenth century, which spring directly from that reformulation – it is most unlikely that all these things in succession and in combination would not have deeply affected the Christian institutions which have had to function throughout under all these immense pressures of history and 'real life'.

I am not trying to suggest that the appeal to history is of no value today in our modern situation, but only that we must cease to use it in this superficial and naïve way. The comparative barrenness of decisive results in the modern study of primitive Church Order is partly explained by the defect in technical historical method which this superficiality involves – by the rigidly 'Constitutional' approach to the evidence and the neglect of all considerations of 'Administrative' realities. In the result all parties to the modern discussions have allowed themselves, when considering the ancient evidence, to be hypnotised by certain words, forgetting that words – even when used as technical terms – can and often do change their whole connotation between one generation and the next in the history of institutions without any breach whatever of institutional continuity . . . The only safeguard against such changes lies in elaborate quasi-legal definitions, of which the primitive Church knew nothing. We shall have to get behind words to the ideas and realities they express, before we can either understand the ancient historical evidence or solve the modern ecclesiastical problem.

It is one primary difference between these that whereas the modern problem has been allowed to revolve almost exclusively around the words 'episcopacy' and 'episcopate', the words *episkopē* and *episkopos* play no significant part whatever in the historical process of the development of the classical Church Order. It would help considerably towards disentangling the discussion if we could all accept the fact that the ancient evidence about *episkopē* and *episkopoi* is largely irrelevant to our own ecclesiastical controversies. From the ancient standpoint there is no 'development of episcopacy', no 'emergence of the episcopate', either at the turn of the first and second centuries or at any other point. *Episkopē* is there from the beginning; it is a necessary function from the start in the corporate life of any *paroikia* or Christian local Church. In the primitive Church *episkopos* is not the title of an 'order' at all. It is a description of anyone who fulfils *episkopē*, applied indiscriminately to those who fulfil it, whether an individual or a college. Just so there was a time when anyone who fulfilled *diakonia* was called *diakonos*. 'Order' and 'function' are not necessarily the same thing in the primitive Church. 'Functions' are many and various, and the equipment for fulfilling them are the *charismata*. The primitive 'orders' are two only – the 'apostles' or *shelihim* and the 'presbyters' or *zeqenim* (supplemented soon by the 'deacons'). It was only the customary discharge of a particular 'function' by a particular 'order' which led in time to a criss-cross use of 'functional' terminology to describe the 'orders', and ultimately to the technical terms we know . . .

Thus the apparent transformation of the 'apostle + presbyter-*episkopoi* + deacons' hierarchy of the first century into the '*episkopos* + presbyters + deacons' hierarchy of the second century does not mask the creation of any new 'order' in the Church. It only records the permanent localisation of the apostle and the consequent permanent transfer to him of a function in the life of the local Church in addition to his own personal commission as the *shaliach* of our Lord. The proof of this is to be found in the treatment of the episcopate in such documents as the *Apostolic Tradition*, at the earliest point at which we can investigate the ancient understanding of the office in any detail. The fact that for a while and in some Churches the exercise of *episkopē* had formerly been committed to a single individual (naturally styled *episkopos*), who was *not* also an 'apostle' but only the president of the local presbytery, is, from the point of view of the modern problem, only an irrelevant and confusing accident; though at the time it may well have hastened and eased the process of fitting the apostle into the life of the local Church. But the ancient constitutional problem and the ancient constitutional history were concerned primarily with the adjustment of the *shaliach* to the *zeqenim*, not with the distribution of functions among the *zeqenim*.

With this in mind let us examine for a moment the terms of the modern problem. It is generally assumed by Anglicans that because our ministry retains the titles of bishop, priest, and deacon, Anglican Church Order reproduces with some exactness the Church Order of Ignatius and Hippolytus. Yet as soon as we get behind the mere identity of words it is obvious that in practical fact it does not. Bishops and presbyters have in large part exchanged functions since the second century, and few modern Anglican dioceses would half expect to find the natural successor to a dead bishop among his clerics in deacon's orders. An infinitesimal proportion of our laity have been baptised by their own bishop, or have even once in their lives made their communion at his hands. The second-century laity expected to do so as a matter of course every Sunday. They had all not only been confirmed by him but baptised by him (or at least in his presence); they were married by him, and if they fell into grave sin were disciplined and absolved by him personally. They expected to be visited by him when they were ill, to be pacified by him if they quarrelled with one another, and buried by him when they died. All this was his *episkopē* – his particular 'function' in the life of his Church. They all expected, too, to have some voice in the selection of his successor. These facts have a vital bearing on the relation of a bishop to his own flock – an important point, surely, in discussing 'episcopacy'. There is a further point of difference, too, between the primitive and the Anglican Church Orders which is of the greatest significance – the virtual atrophy amongst us of the bishop's doctrinal *magisterium*, his function as the supernaturally endowed and authoritative 'witness' to authentic Christian doctrine. The pre-Nicene bishop was recognised to have a special *charisma*, a 'prophetic' function of accurately voicing dogmatic truth according to the tradition of that particular local society to which he and his fellows all belonged; and none of his laity or presbyters could believe otherwise without at least the presumption of pride and heresy. What does this mean for us? Does even the firmest Anglican believer in the Apostolic Succession today base, *e.g.*, his own Eucharistic doctrine first of all upon the fact that this is exactly what his own bishop teaches? Yet Irenaeus, for instance, expects the presbyters and laity of his own day to reject Gnosticism, primarily because it is opposed by the teaching authority of their own bishops.

We Anglicans may say, if we like, that we have retained the pre-Nicene institution of 'episcopacy', but let us be clear also that its functions are mostly no longer exercised in practice by the 'episcopate', which is now primarily an organising and administrative office discharging functions once exercised by the pre-Nicene college of presbyters. We recognise this fact, indeed, in our terminology. Our word for the bishop's sphere is not the pre-Nicene *paroikia* or 'parish',[A] but the later term of secular and bureaucratic origin – *dioikēsis* or 'diocese', meaning an administrative subdivision of a centralised system of government from above. The change of term, which begins only in the seventh-eighth century, is not without significance. We have kept 'bishops', but in our 'dioceses' we have virtually abolished the organic life of self-contained local societies, each with a vital definable 'tradition' of its own in liturgy, doctrine, and discipline, in continual contact and interplay with other similar traditions in other similar societies, yet each in many ways autarchic and free to enrich itself and develop along its own lines from within. But it was this system which gave much of its meaning to pre-Nicene 'episcopacy'.

Again, the presbyters of one of our dioceses are no longer the corporate organ and guardian of an intense corporate local life of this kind. They have no corporate status at all or means of corporate expression as the presbyters of a particular bishop's *sanhedrin*.

Instead they are a congeries of individuals collected from without as well as within the diocesan boundaries; each has an individual right, dependent on the personal possession of holy orders but acquired from all sorts of different sources (by presentation), to perform in a particular locality certain liturgical and pastoral functions which in the pre-Nicene Church were the special responsibility of the bishop and deacons. What else does this mean but that in our system what the pre-Nicene church called *episkopē* and *diakonia* have largely been transferred to the 'parish priest' (and his assistants, who are not encouraged to remain deacons longer than they can help).

I am not in the least contending that we should return to the primitive system, but that in our discussions on Church Order we should cease to be hypnotised by the *words* bishop, presbyter, and deacon, and get down to the realities. Whatever our 'Constitutional' continuity with the ancient ministry, no one can or ought in the face of 'Administrative' changes of such magnitude to pretend that the Anglican Church perpetuates the pre-Nicene Church Order. We perpetuate, instead, that drastic modification of it which was reached in the fourth century, as further greatly modified by irrelevant feudal accretions during the Middle Ages, and still further removed from the original by the debasements of Christian practice introduced by Tudor and Stuart lawyers. It can only bring devastating confusion into the question of Reunion to set up such an historical amalgam in its present working as a model principle, and attempt to impose it on others merely because it retains a few ancient technical terms.

Now let us look at the other side of the question. We should all be a long step nearer agreement if we recognised that the modern Protestant Societies cannot be 'given' or 'asked to accept' *episkopē* in the ancient sense at all, because they already have it. It is an inseparable accompaniment of any corporate Christian life, and the Protestant ministries have had every right to be suspicious of our attempts to thrust a merely 'Administrative' episcopate upon them, as casting doubts upon the reality of their own ministerial office. All the Reformed ministries of the sixteenth century reproduced, at least in intention and function, the primitive *zeqenim* of the local Churches, as these would have been had there never been any 'apostolate' . . .

With the recognition of these facts we are in a position to effect one great clarification in the modern problem of Christian Union. What is really in question in our present discussions about 'episcopacy' is not the 'episcopate' at all. It is the 'apostolate'. There is no way of avoiding that fact. Even that unhappy phrase 'the historic episcopate', with which well-meaning ecclesiastical diplomats have sought so earnestly to unite us all by a misunderstanding, proves at this point quite unhelpful to their purpose. The trouble is not that it is ambiguous or even quite meaningless, but that it cannot be employed in our present difficulty without at once becoming either obviously untrue or else dangerously intelligible. What in history can it possibly mean? The mere concentration of *episkopē* in the hands of a single member of the local ministry *without* the personal commission of the *shaliach* – a sort of antiquarian revival of the office of Diotrephes? Then it is not the 'historic' episcopate at all which is intended, but the 'pre-historic' one, an attempted resurrection of a fossil species long ago extinct. Or is it that, as we are told, 'The historic episcopate means the episcopate which has existed since the latter half of the second century in the whole Church till the sixteenth, and since then in the largest part of Christendom'?[B] That is certainly 'historic' enough; but historically it is clear to demonstration from Hippolytus that 'in the latter half of the second century' this meant only the apostolate fulfilling certain functions in a local Church, and that has certainly been understood to be its meaning all over Christendom ever since. Thus this question-begging phrase fails to achieve its object of avoiding the main question at issue. Those who accept the 'historic episcopate' are placed in the position of accepting with it the apostolate, unless they positively declare that they exclude such an interpretation. And if they do that, then the 'episcopate' they do accept ceases *ipso facto* to be 'historic' in any ascertainable sense of the word.

It may be said that this insufficiently recognises the diplomatic value of the phrase, which has as a matter of fact allowed us to make clear that we do for our own part semi-officially reserve the right to interpret the acceptance of the historic 'episcopate' as involving in itself the 'apostolate', even while we insist also that 'the acceptance of Episcopal ordination does not involve the acceptance of any particular theory of its nature or origin'. By 'theory' here is presumably meant 'doctrine'. Nobody would worry about 'theories'. It is only 'doctrines' which can effectively divide Christians. But quite apart from this not altogether innocent little piece of verbal *camouflage*, it is to be feared that those whom it is hoped thus to lure into unity with one another will on both sides detect the entire unreality from their own point of view of the settlement which is suggested.

From the Catholic standpoint the complaint would run something like this: 'What *could* be meant by "the historic episcopate" apart from one particular "theory" of its nature and origin? How could anyone possibly bring under the heading of a single historical institution embodiments so diverse as the pre-Nicene bishop, with his strong resemblance to the elected city-magistrate of antiquity; the hereditary patriarch of the Assyrian Church; the imperially-nominated Byzantine spiritual bureaucrat; the ordaining bishop of the Celtic Churches, without see or jurisdiction; the prince-bishop of the Middle Ages; the solitary bishop (*abouna*) of the Abyssinian Church, always a foreigner ordained abroad and under oath never to consecrate anyone to the episcopate; the Tudor or Stuart functionary in episcopal orders whose principal *raison d'être* was to administer certain Acts of Parliament for the Uniformity of Religion – how could one possibly bring all these and other equally variant manifestations of the episcopate under a single heading apart from the single similarity, that each in its own age and place was regarded as the unique depositary or embodiment of the apostolic office and power to ordain? Apart from that "particular theory of its origin and nature" there is simply no such thing as "the historic episcopate" at all, but only an endlessly varying series of different arrangements for Church government, which have not even all used the same titles and technical terms. That "theory" is a part, the essential and major part and the only universal part, of the "history" of the episcopate, because it has informed and moulded that whole history. Without it, the proposed "episcopate" is not "historic" at all – but simply the present Anglican machinery of Church administration imposed upon other people as a means of unifying organisations, but without the only existing justification for that machine, the only link with the apostolic pattern which that organisation still at present retains. If you deny that that link is necessary or that it even exists, then the only reason why we still felt it necessary to cling to that system at all costs, even in its degradation, has been removed.'

On the other hand, from the Protestant standpoint the situation is no less impossible, though the complaint would be differently framed. 'Granted that we are not required verbally to affirm the doctrine of the Apostolic Succession, which we totally reject and disbelieve, we are in fact being committed to acting upon it. The moment you absolutely *restrict the act of ordination* to bishops, you do in effect raise the whole question of the difference between the primitive *shaliach* and the primitive *zeqenim*. That was precisely the chief difference of function between them so far as concerned the inner life of individual local Churches. It is no use saying that you only so restrict it out of deference to the example of "the Church in the latter part of the second century", and not of the Church of the apostolic age, because we know now why ordination was restricted to bishops in the second century. It was just because bishops then were supposed to be "apostles" in a sense that other ministers were not. Unless we are allowed publicly and formally to *repudiate* the precedent of "the Church in the latter part of the second century" we shall in fact be betraying our most vital principle of ministry.'

Both protests are entirely justified, and it is impossible to say which side would be committing the greater sin against the light as they see it if they accepted such an arrangement. What the Catholic ministries claim to possess and what the Protestant ministries disclaimed and repudiated of set purpose from the beginning, is a direct and formal continuance among them of that personal commission which was bestowed by our Lord upon His apostles, a commission which the Church at large cannot bestow but must recognise. Here, and not in any boggling over 'the historic episcopate' viewed purely as an administrative system, is the root of the modern difficulty. It has no counterpart at all in antiquity. The relation of the *shaliach* to the *zeqenim* might be quite undefined; there might be questions raised as to who had and who had not received the commission of the *shaliach*, as in the case of St Paul. But the *fact* that some Christian ministers had received it and others had not was nowhere denied. The modern controversies over 'Apostolic Succession' have centred almost entirely upon the episcopate, but the question has in reality much wider implications than this. Through the extension by delegation of so large a part of the properly 'episcopal' functions to the priesthood, it now involves the whole nature of the Christian ministry, its function and authority, and not merely the administrative and ordaining functions of the 'episcopate' strictly so called. To both parties to the dispute this difference is vital, and it must be stated briefly.

It is common ground to all Catholics and all those Protestants who still believe in the atonement that the personal relation of Jesus of Nazareth both to God and to all other men cannot be fully stated only in terms of the office of a Prophet, nor yet even in terms only of Messiahship, of God's 'Anointed' King over all mankind. It must also be described as being without qualification 'priestly'. He is 'Priest', exhausting in Himself the whole meaning of the word, just as He manifests and indeed is the whole revelation of God as Prophet – 'the Word'; just as He is the originating Head of the whole redeemed race as 'the Second Adam', in whom all His posterity are in some sort contained. He is these things with a plenitude which knows no limitations; in no way do they depend upon human acknowledgement of them for their validity. Thus He is 'Priest' not only by office but by nature, right down to the substance of His Being. He is not *a* Priest, even in the sense that the Father could choose Him for this out of a number of possible competitors; still less by human election, as though mankind had selected Him from among themselves to represent them before God. He is *the* Priest, inevitably, because of what He is, Very God and Very Man, the Mediator. He at once glorifies and propitiates God and atones for other men's sins by His own latreutic and sacrificial action. That, and nothing less than that, is 'Priesthood' according to New Testament teaching.

By *nature* it is His alone. The question is whether by *office* He can clothe His Priesthood upon other men. It was the original intention of the Societies which sprang from the Protestant Reformation to continue to attach this conception to our Lord Himself and indeed to re-emphasise it with all their power. But they denied emphatically that He could or did bestow it upon other men even as an office. In their conception of the ministry they repudiated not only all forms of 'sacerdotalism' in the mediaeval sense, but every notion that He could or did impart to any other men a *right* to stand before God in His Person for their fellows, or before their fellows in His Person for God. In other words, they denied the possibility of the commission of the *shaliach* – 'for a man's *shaliach* is as it were himself'. It was this whole aspect of the traditional ministry – not of the episcopate only, but of the other orders also insofar as it had since the fourth century come to be attached to them – which they were determined altogether to exclude from their own ministries for the future. It was for this reason that they repudiated the traditional titles and structure of the ministry, and in many cases reordained Catholic priests who were converted to Protestantism. They did not claim continuity or even parity with the past. They intended to substitute for it something which they conceived to be better, and which was at least wholly and designedly different. These are indisputable facts.

Here, then, is a cardinal point of difference between ancient precedents and the modern situation. We can and should allow that the Protestant ministries reproduce in essence and function the primitive local ministry of the *zeqenim* for their own Societies. But that does not mean that the mere superimposition upon them of a 'diocesan' organisation with administrators and 'ordainers' termed 'bishops' will restore the ancient situation. The form taken by the Protestant ministries in the sixteenth century not only overturned

the ancient solution of the abstract 'constitutional' problem of adjusting the unrelated institutions of the *shaliach* and the *zeqenim*, which
was gradually worked out between *c.* A.D. 50 and *c.* A.D. 350. It
went further, and denied that the ancient problem had ever existed. It
eliminated one factor of that problem altogether, and that the factor
which was of directly Dominical institution, framing its own solution
in terms only of the ecclesiastical factor. The problem of reuniting the
Catholic and Protestant conceptions of the ministry does not reopen
the ancient problem as it stood *c.* A.D. 350 or even *c.* A.D. 50. It
opens another question altogether – whether the Lord's commission
to His *shelihim* played any legitimate part at all in the formation of
the permanent Christian ministry.

Catholicism and Protestantism return different answers to that.
But neither answer was elaborated on the basis of a critical examination of the early evidence. The permanent Christian ministry
grew up in unbroken continuity from both elements in the primitive organisation, and the Catholic doctrine merely rationalised the
historical facts. The Protestant answer was formulated long afterwards, but quite without reference to the essential historical evidence.
It was only a logical deduction from and application of the dogma of
'Justification by faith alone'; and anyone who cares to examine the
earliest statements on the ministry by Luther and Zwingli will find
that it is actually put forward as such. It is a mistake to suppose that
it was the 'corruptions' of the early sixteenth-century hierarchy which
brought about the Protestant rejection of it; though the corruptions
were undoubtedly there to a considerable extent, and no doubt added
point and impetus to that rejection. But it should be obvious to anyone considering the implications of the doctrine of 'Justification by
faith alone', which all the Protestant leaders again and again insisted
was the *punctum stantis vel cadentis ecclesiae*, that those who held
it were bound to reject the Catholic hierarchy, at least in the Catholic
understanding of it, even if all its members then had been angels in
human form.[c]

Where the doctrine of 'Justification by faith alone' is held, no question of Church Order can be anything but entirely secondary, even
meaningless. No external institution of any kind can ever be regarded
as in itself *necessary* for the living of the redeemed life. The commission of the *shaliach* could no more be looked upon as necessary to
the corporate life of Christians than baptism could be supposed
'generally necessary for salvation' for Christian individuals.

Here is a topic about which our discussions on Reunion have

been most noticeably silent. Yet it was a difference upon this and not upon organisation which split Western Christendom in the sixteenth century. In fact, some who retained the ancient organisation but accepted the new doctrine (*e.g.* in Sweden) nevertheless departed from the ancient unity, and preferred the communion of those who had abandoned the old organisation to that of those who had kept it. Can we afford to ignore altogether the root cause of all our divisions? It is more than a difference upon a point of doctrine. It is a difference about the nature of man's fall and the process of his union with God; that is, it is admittedly a difference about the very notion of 'religion' itself. Where that exists, discussion of the early evidence on the nature and form of the Christian ministry is hardly much more than a scholarly amusement. Until that fundamental division has been faced and agreement sought on that – who of those in authority has seriously attempted to do so in modern times? – to try to base union on details of organisation and phrases about the 'historic episcopate' is to try to bind the broken fragments of Christendom with ropes of sand. We once had a common organisation and shared the 'historic episcopate'. But when that major difference declared itself it split us asunder as easily as a wedge splits wood; and it has kept us apart ever since – for all our differences as between Protestant and Catholic spring ultimately directly from that.

History, indeed, has a further warning for the advocates of the 'historic episcopate' divorced from 'theories' as an administrative solution of troublesome dogmatic differences. Elsewhere in this book the staunchness of sixteenth- and seventeenth-century Anglicans in upholding episcopacy receives a proper emphasis. The other side of the matter is that over-emphasis on the 'historic' claim of episcopacy to the neglect of the 'theory' of it once brought England to civil war. The treatment of the Puritans by the English episcopate from the reign of Elizabeth onwards must be sorrowfully admitted to have been as stupid as it was Erastian and wicked, whatever the provocation of factiousness on the other side. Bating, of course, the seventeenth-century emphasis on the statutory powers of bishops, in what did episcopacy as advocated by Bancroft[1] or by Bishop Parker of Oxford[2] in his *Discourse of Ecclesiastical Policie* (1670) differ essentially from the recommendations of it in these current proposals? It is strange indeed to find this conception advocated now as by itself a sufficient remedy for the very troubles it once inflamed. There is no schism in the history of English religion from Whitgift to Wesley in which episcopal administrators standing on their 'historic' position instead of on their apostolic charge have not played the part of Amaziah the priest of Bethel: 'O thou prophet, go flee thee away into the land of Judah, and there eat bread and prophesy there: but prophesy not any more at Bethel: for this is the King's chapel and this is the court of the King.' (Amos 7.12) It may be said that there is small probability that Anglican bishops today would repeat this policy with Puritan Dissenters, and one hopes indeed that they would not. But is it quite certain that none of them would be prepared to follow it in the case of the modern representatives of the Caroline divines?

If the best that could truthfully be said for episcopacy from the ancient evidence were that it is 'historic', that it has been going on for a very long while, then its acceptance in the form we Anglicans know it certainly could not be rightly made an *essential* of unity with other Christians. After all, as much could be said for any long-standing abuse. No one could have any right to make this particular administrative device a *sine qua non* of Christian unity, any more than, say, archdeacons, who also make their appearance in the latter part of the second century. It is not its history, which is not without its repulsive aspects, but its apostolicity which – in spite of its history – makes episcopacy in some form candidly defensible as the optimum system of Church Order. The episcopate is the only means by which our Lord's own commission to stand in His Person before God and man is given afresh to each new minister of His Church (according to His own order) to the end of time. Apart from that 'theory' – or rather fact – episcopacy has no particular meaning and need not be treated as anything but an administrative convenience, to be retained or abandoned or bargained about as occasion may serve.

But if once that fact were effectively safeguarded, it is hard to think of any concession in the matter of Church Order which Catholics could not or ought not to make for the sake of unity, or of any tempo-rary anomaly which they ought not gladly and charitably to tolerate for the sake of that overmastering end. The Church is not irrevocably bound to the fourth-century embodiment of this perpetual (because Dominically instituted) principle which Catholicism has preserved, as, *e.g.*, the later history of the episcopate in the Celtic Churches shows. Still less is it bound to those later modifications and obscur-ings of it under which the Church of England at present exists. But without the clear acknowledgement of the necessity of that apostolic commission, which for us happens to be bound up with the diocesan episcopate, there would not in fact be any union of the Catholic and Protestant conceptions of the ministry at all. What would have been lost from the resulting amalgam, even though it were still governed by 'bishops', would be precisely that historic element of the Christian ministry which Protestantism originally discarded and Catholicism has retained from the Church Order of the apostolic age – the Lord's commission to His *shelihim* to act not only in His Name but in His Person – 'for a man's *shaliach* is as it were himself'.

(*MEC* 288, 290–303)

### Notes

A. Whether *paroikia* in Christian usage derived from the customary Greek sense of a group of neighbours, or retained something of its special Septuagint meaning of a group of 'sojourners' or aliens resident in a foreign land (whose true home was in heaven), makes no difference to the fact that paroikia, 'parish', or ekklēsia, 'Church', are the only terms for a pre-Nicene bishop's sphere of function.

B. Dr. E. J. Palmer, sometime Bishop of Bombay and from 1919 to 1929 a Member of the Joint Committee on Church Union in South India, in *South India: The Meaning of the Scheme*, 1944, p. 13.

C. Witness, e.g., the Lutheran Episcopal Church in Sweden, in full communion with non-episcopal Lutheran Churches, though itself, as one of its bishops has claimed, retaining the Apostolic Succession, but 'as though we possessed it not'.

1. John Bancroft (1574–1641), Bishop of Oxford.
2. Samuel Parker (1640–1688), Bishop of Oxford.

## The Fourth Century: a Turning Point for Episcopacy

*In a series of seven articles which appeared in* Laudate *in 1937 and 1938, Dix responds to B. J. Kidd's* The Roman Primacy to A.D. 461 *(SPCK, 1936). In this passage Dix argues that the Church's understanding of the role of the bishop undergoes a fundamental shift in the fourth century, from sacramental 'order' to juridical 'office', thereby impoverishing the Church's self-understanding as the Body of Christ.*

It is, I think, possible to show that during the fourth century a very considerable change took place in the relation of the local bishop to his Church, and above all in the way in which that relation was regarded both by bishops and their flocks. It is not merely a change of language, though that is noticeable. From being the "leader" and "president" of a "*Church*" the bishop became the "ruler" of a "*diocese*" (with its implications of a secular government) and a "territory". There does develop a partly new technical vocabulary to describe the bishop's authority, and a new regalism of language about bishops which carries new implications. But this only represents a much more important shift of emphasis in the conception of the episcopate, from the sacramentally bestowed charismatic endowment of an "Order" to the juridically bestowed power of an "Office." Both elements had always been there to some extent in the bishop's authority. But before the fourth century one was predominant, and after it the other. In the result there is all the difference between authority *in* the Church and an authority *over* it. It is a change which can be watched taking place simultaneously in other departments of the Church's life; it alters, for instance, the relation of the eucharistic celebrant to the worshippers. At the beginning of the third century the eucharist is recognized to be a corporate act of the whole Church as the "Body of Christ," in which every "order," bishop, presbyters, deacons, laity, have each their own organic function, and which *requires* the co-operation of every order for its completion. By the end of the fourth century it is becoming almost everywhere (what in the general conception still remains) something done *by* the clergy (and chiefly the celebrant or celebrants) *for* the laity, whose only function is to look on.

This universal shifting of emphasis in the conception of the Church seems to have passed unrecognized at the time. There are virtually no protests or reactions. Old forms continue everywhere, though with a changing meaning. Its completion is symbolized by the substitution of the new conception of a written *statute* Canon Law for the old *customary* Canon Law of pre-Nicene days, which takes place everywhere more or less at the same time, *c.* A.D. 390–410. To indicate only one aspect of the importance of this: Custom recognized as binding can only change slowly by the common change of mind of all concerned; statute law changes by the decision of an accepted law-giver. What is involved in the whole process is nothing less than a re-writing of the old conception of Church in a quite new "juridical" idiom. And among other old things then re-written in that new idiom is, it seems to me, the position of the Papacy.

In the case of the local bishop's relation to his Church, it is an exaggeration to regard the process as one which gave him powers which he had never had before. But he will exercise them hereafter by a different title in a different way. Effective "leadership" will always produce much the same results as juridical authority, probably in a better way. In retrospect its action may well look very like authority; the will of the "leader" is in fact what "gets done", often as smoothly as though he had an admitted right to command. And there had always been aspects of the bishop's office which encouraged such a conception. The change to the new juridical conception is simply that these aspects replace the old charismatic endowment of his order as the *foundation* of his authority. From being a sacramental person who alone is empowered by God at the Church's prayer to perform certain necessary "liturgies" of the "Body of Christ" in "the Church that sojourneth at" X, and in consequence is the "leader" and "guide" of all the Christians there both as individuals and corporately, the bishop becomes the official who has authority over all the Christians in X, and as such has the duty and privilege of performing either in person or by a deputy (who does *not* derive "jurisdiction" from this) all the sacramental functions needed among them. The sacramental power to perform them is still conveyed by the Sacrament of Order. But jurisdiction and order are now separate things, and it is jurisdiction that is the novelty. What has been impoverished is not the notion of the Episcopate as such, but the notion of the Church as the "Body of Christ."

(JEC 17–19)

## Apostolic Succession

*This passage comes from a paper entitled 'Holy Order' which Dix read to a Priests' Convention in the United States in 1950 and which was published posthumously in 1976. Although the majority of scholars no longer hold to the belief that the* Apostolic Tradition *is a single-author work which can be dated to around* AD 215, *this does not diminish Dix's argument that 'apostolic simultaneity' may be a more helpful way of understanding apostolic succession.*

The episcopate has been challenged on many grounds – that it is unhistorical, that it is magical, that it unduly limits God to human means, and so on. There have indeed been those who have maintained that Jesus of Nazareth had no intention of founding any permanent Church, or *a fortiori* organizing any permanent ministry, even that of the Apostles themselves. Let us, however, without seeking to make a special answer to each of these various objections, try to make a positive presentation to ourselves of what the doctrine means, in the light of objective historical facts.

In first-century Palestine any Messianic movement of any kind which looked for the coming of the Kingdom of God in any form was bound to envisage the renewed Israel, the purified People of God, as the subject and sphere of that kingship. In that form the Church is certainly of our Lord's design . . .

And around our Lord, in all our oldest historical sources, there are two concentric groups, 'the disciples' in general ('about an hundred and twenty persons' in Acts 1) and 'the Twelve' or 'the Apostles'. And all our sources are clear that originally the principle of demarcation between them rested on our Lord's own appointment. 'He went up into a mountain and called unto him whom he would; and he made twelve, whom also he called apostles.' (Mark 3.13f.; Luke 6.13) Even if we admit for purposes of argument, as has been alleged, that the title 'Apostles' is a later invention, the appointment by our Lord of the Twelve is not a later gloss upon the facts. Our earliest Christian documents, coming from a source which had every motive to challenge the fact of that appointment if it were untrue, show clearly that it was common knowledge in the first Christian generation that the Twelve owed their position, whatever it was, to our Lord's own action. St Paul's passionate and repeated claim, when the Twelve or others for them would have questioned his own position as an Apostle, is that he, too, owed his own appointment to precisely the same source as their own; it was the weakness of his position that he could not, like them, produce witnesses. Some sort of ministry, therefore, in his future Church is of our Lord's own design.

What then was the Apostles' position in the eyes of the earliest Church? Three of the Gospels are unanimous that the corporate Apostolate was regarded as a permanent replacement on earth of our Lord himself. They place upon his lips such far-reaching phrases as 'He that receiveth you receiveth me'. (Mt. 11.40) 'Lo I am with you always, even unto the end of the world'. (Mt. 28.20) 'I appoint unto you a kingship just as my Father hath appointed unto me'. (Luke 22.29) 'Receive the Holy Ghost' (*i.e.* that Messianic 'Spirit of the Lord' in virtue of which he *is* Messiah, and the 'Servant' of Isaiah 42.1) – 'As my Father hath sent me, even so send I you'. (John 22.21f.) And the other Gospel, St Mark's, seems to be incomplete at the point at which other evidence would lead us to expect some such charge, in the resurrection appearances. Here is the nucleus and charter of the Christian hierarchy, a permanent and apparently unlimited commission to act in our Lord's Name, which in Semitic ideas means in *his Person.*

Archbishop Benson[1] once remarked that 'The Apostolic Succession is not a doctrine, it is a fact.' However brief a while the Apostles may originally have supposed their tenure of this authority in this world would last, it is a fact that they held it until their deaths and that other men succeeded to their position when they died. We have excellent historical evidence for this in the letter written by Clement of Rome to the Corinthians in A.D. 96. In a famous passage he affirms unequivocally that they themselves in the end made arrangements about this, and implies that there were still living at Corinth men who had been appointed by the Apostles themselves or by men whom they had appointed to succeed them. (1 Clement 44) The 'succession' is not peculiar to Rome and Corinth; it is a fact of universal application, of his correspondents' own knowledge, to which he appeals in order to convince people who would have some reason to resent his letter, and every reason to contradict him or at least to refuse to do as he wished if his facts were wrong. He is writing about a generation after the deaths of Ss Peter and Paul, the Apostles both of Rome and of Corinth. If his own Christian recollection did not reach back as far as their times (and the leader of the Roman Christians was not likely to be either a young man or a neophyte) still there would be some whose memory did go back. This very letter is to be 'conveyed by three messengers, faithful and prudent men that have walked among us from youth unto old age unblameably.' (1 Clement 43.3) It is inconceivable that Clement should have misreported the facts as to a deliberate appointment of 'successors' by Apostles at Rome and Corinth alike, and we need not look for further evidence.

Though he is clear as to the 'appointment' of successors by the Apostles, Clement says nothing as to an 'ordination' of these successors with the laying on of hands, and it is quite conceivable, though perhaps not altogether probable, that this did not take place. Such an ordination was in use in the Judaic surroundings in which the Church first arose, and appears definitely established in the Christian church by the end of the first century. But in the earliest instances of which we know, the fullness of the commission to act in our Lord's Person is regarded as being extended beyond the survivors of the Twelve, not by their own action, but rather by an act of appointment by the Risen Lord himself, similar to that by which the Twelve had been appointed. Certainly the appointment of St Matthias in Acts 1 is to be so regarded. The Church puts forward two men who are suitable, and the outcome of the sacred lot is taken as indicating our Lord's own appointment. There is no other ordination, but simply the statement that Matthias 'was numbered with the eleven', in consequence of our Lord's own choice. So also it is with St Paul, and probably with St James the Just[A] and St Barnabas. In the 2nd or 3rd Christian generation St Timothy's ordination is represented as first ordered by prophecy (*i.e.* by the command of our Lord, given through a prophet) and then accomplished by the laying on of hands. (1 Tim. 4.14) This represents a stage half-way between the original conception and the later practice.

It is impossible here to go into all the intricacies of the historical evidence concerning the ministry which comes from the two or three generations immediately succeeding this earliest period, nor is it necessary. Such questions as whether the original 'successors' appointed by the Apostles took the form of a collegiate authority rather than a single individual in particular churches do not affect the principle of such a 'succession', which is what we are concerned with. Suffice it that episcopacy in a form recognizably that which we know is found everywhere by a date about A.D. 150. Let us now take a jump to the next undisputedly solid piece of evidence and examine the earliest account we have of a bishop's consecration, which is found in the *Apostolic Tradition*, written by St Hippolytus, at Rome *c.* 215 A.D. Here the Church elects a candidate, as in the case of St Matthias. Then the bishops of the neighbouring Churches lay hands upon him, praying in silence 'for the descent of the Spirit'. Finally one bishop alone, laying a hand on his head, prays thus:

' . . . Now pour forth that power which is from thee of the princely Spirit (*or* 'Spirit of leadership') which thou didst deliver to thy Beloved Servant Jesus Christ, which he bestowed upon thy Holy Apostles who established in every place the Church which hallows thee . . .

Grant upon this thy servant, whom thou hast chosen for the episcopate to shepherd thy holy flock and to be high-priest unto thee, that he may liturgize blamelessly by night and day; that he may ceaselessly propitiate thy Countenance and offer to thee the gifts of thy holy Church; and that by the high-priestly Spirit he may have authority to forgive sins according to thy command, to 'give lots' (? ordain clergy) according to thy bidding, to loose every bond according to the authority thou gavest to the Apostles . . .'.
(*Apostolic Tradition* 2 and 3)

There are certain points here which require attention. (a) This prayer gives no support to that quite modern notion of the Apostolic Succession as a mere transmission of the Spirit once for all received by the Apostles and ever after handed on from ordainers to ordained by the contact of their hands – 'like a contagion', as Mgr Knox[2] once said. It is a fresh act of the power of God which is here contemplated. '*Now* pour forth . . .' (b) What is here sought for the elect is that *same* Messianic 'Spirit of the Lord' which 'thou didst deliver to thy Beloved Servant Jesus Christ, which he bestowed on thy Apostles . . .' (We are here in contact with very primitive ideas and terminology indeed. This is quite unlike Hippolytus' own Christology). (c) The choice of the elect is still regarded as the direct act *of God himself.* 'Whom *thou* hast chosen for the episcopate.' (d) 'the episcopate' involves acting as the Good Shepherd and High Priest, the functions of our Lord himself. (e) It is only by possession of (or 'by') the 'High-Priestly Spirit' that the bishop fulfils his liturgical and sacramental functions, *i.e.* the bishop's ministry in its most sacerdotal aspect is essentially a 'charismatic ministry' to use a modern term.

I do not see how we are to avoid the conclusion that there is in this prayer a deliberate identifying of the episcopate with the apostolate in its spiritual endowment and responsibilities, and an equating of the whole corporate apostolate (*i.e.* apostolate *plus* episcopate) with our Lord. I am the more convinced this is its true interpretation in that the same author in another work speaks of the episcopate as 'successors of the Apostles and *sharers* with them of the *same* charisma of high-priesthood and teaching authority.' (*Philosophumena* C1) It would be hard to state the identity of the Apostolic and episcopal vocations more plainly.

If we try to analyse the conception of ordination here implied, we must conclude that it is still essentially the same as that to be found in Acts. The consecration of a new bishop is still the aggregating of one more member to the original Apostolic college by the choice and act of appointment by our Lord *himself.* Only now the action of him invisibly present has come to be expressed outwardly by the imposition of the hands of those whom our Lord has already called and commissioned to act in *his Person*, after the fashion already found in the later documents of the New Testament. Just as the consecration of every Eucharist by an earthly celebrant involves his act as Priest, because it is *anamnesis* – the 're-calling', in the sense of making here and now present and operative in its effects – of his sacrifice, so every episcopal consecration is the *anamnesis* of his original act calling and commissioning Apostles.

In one sense this presents us with a doctrine not so much of the Apostolic Succession as of 'Apostolic Simultaneity' of all bishops. It is a peculiarly vivid way of envisaging that unity of the ministry which is the single earthly instrument of the organic life of the whole timeless Body of Christ. Of course 'succession language' has to be used of what occurs in the temporal order. But it is of importance to note that in the 2nd century the 'succession' denotes not, as in our thought, the *sacramental* succession to the episcopate received by a bishop from those bishops who consecrate him. It is used exclusively of his *historical* succession to his own dead predecessors in his own see – and so, eventually, back to those first 'bishops, to whom' – as the later second century unanimously asserted – 'the apostles entrusted the several churches'. (Irenaeus, *Against Heresies*, 5.20.1) There are thus *two* distinct things, on this view, necessary to make a man truly the organ of the whole Body of Christ in the exercise of the episcopate: (a) In the temporal order, the acceptance of him in the life of the Church *i.e.* a rightful succession to predecessors, conveyed to him by the free choice of those predecessors' own flock; (b) In the supernatural order, our Lord's own action in adding him to the one ever-growing college of Apostles, conveyed to him by the sacramental action of those whom one Lord has already commissioned to act in his Person, *i.e.* by ordination at the hands of other bishops. So conceived, the Apostolic Succession is certainly not fairly open to the charge of 'magical' conceptions.

(*HO* 11–16)

### Notes

A. The 2nd century tradition represented by the *Gospel according to the Hebrews*, Hegesippus and Clement of Alexandria, suggests this appointment by our Lord after the resurrection. Later tradition attributes it to the Apostles.

1. Edward Benson (1829–96) was Archbishop of Canterbury from 1883 until his death.

2. Ronald Knox (1888–1957) was a convert to Roman Catholicism from Anglicanism.

# The Question of Anglican Orders: Letters to a Layman

*As an Anglo-Papalist whose spiritual life and that of his community were formed and sustained by the rites of the Roman Catholic Church, the question of the validity of Anglican orders was one which vexed Dix throughout his life and, at times, led him to consider whether his own priesthood should be exercised in communion with Rome. First published in 1944, Dix's popular collection of letters to a layman contain, in Dix's own words, 'the substance of correspondence actually sent to more than one lay person, but not intended for publication at the time'. The two letters reproduced here constitute the first and last of the collection.*

Nashdom Abbey
Burnham, Bucks.
18. xi. '43

My dear Harry, Thank you for your letter and the enclosure. I am truly sorry to hear you are in such distress about it all, though I am not altogether surprised that such happenings have turned your mind towards Rome. I always thought it a pity they should have allowed this South Indian Scheme with its obviously controversial proposals to come to a head in the middle of a war, when everyone is much too distracted and busy to think clearly about it or even to give it any proper attention at all. But still I don't really see how the behaviour of the Upper House of Convocation can be supposed to cast much new light on the validity of Anglican Orders – that endless wrangle! – all the same. It is rather surprising that Father O'Dwyer set off along that line. After all, it is a commonplace of Church history that Bishops of the most ironclad validity have frequently behaved in a queer fashion before now – as it is a matter merely of observation that Christian Ministers who would not claim to be in any sort of Apostolic Succession frequently behave with great holiness and wisdom. St Peter himself and St Barnabas bewildered themselves into behaviour which St Paul describes with obvious self-restraint as 'dissembling' (Gal. 2) over a matter which closely concerned the Faith, as well as the whole practical future of the Christian religion. After such a *contretemps* as that we shall hardly be dismayed beyond hope by the sort of thing which sometimes happens to our own Bishops when they are in a hurry.

The two questions are quite separate: (1) Are our Bishops and Priests really Bishops and Priests? (2) Are they always wise and faithful? The answer 'Yes' to the first no more commits us to the same answer to the second than the answer 'No' would commit us to the theory that they were all invariably and *ex officio* wicked and foolish. They have to be answered on quite different grounds – and by different people. You and I have not to judge the consciences of Anglican Bishops (do let us remember that!). But I suppose that once the first question has been raised clearly in one's own mind we all of us have to reach some sort of decision about it – even if only the practical decision to stay in the C. of E. or to leave it.

I don't quite know what to say about your request for 'help' about this. To be frank, I am not at all flattered by your saying that while I 'can tolerate the C. of E.' you suppose you ought to, too. My being an Anglican is no better a reason for your being one than O'Dwyer's being a Roman is for your becoming one. As it happens I don't 'tolerate the C. of E.' at all. I believe in it – which is quite a different thing – I believe in it sincerely and, I hope, for intelligent reasons, but at bottom probably rather passionately. It isn't just a matter of 'staying where you are because nothing else seems quite decisively better', as you put it. That might do for a temporary anchorage, but conditional loyalties weary a man's heart in the end. Hereditary attachment has a real claim upon *pietas* and affection, and we have a right to let it weigh with us, but only up to a certain point, if we have capacity and opportunity to form an objective judgement on other grounds. It can't alter *facts*. Nor could I personally cling to the C. of E. only or chiefly because of the singular graciousness and goodness of some aspects of its past. They are there, and the 'nobility' of mind which is the special mark of the seventeenth century and the Cavalier ideal has a haunting charm. But these things *are* now in the past, you know! If we face the facts, the C. of E. has changed a great deal in the last forty years, and much of the change consists precisely in the shedding of most of the relics of this tradition. We may well regret it. Even when the stately summer of the Carolines was over, the 'Whig grandee' Bishops of the eighteenth century and the 'Greek Play' Bishops of eighty years ago still had something for which the genial energy of a business man in gaiters does not always quite compensate. It was a dignified tradition, with much of solid good about it, in spite of its gaps. But the growing poverty of the clergy and the growth of great industrial dioceses have today made it permanently impossible to maintain something which was more a consequence of the social 'set-up' based on landed property in the aristocratic rural England of the seventeenth-eighteenth centuries than a product of Anglicanism in itself. And the loss of the old *otium cum dig.* has brought with it a lowering of the general level of clerical scholarship, which counted for a good deal in the building up of that particular tradition.

No, my dear man! If you are only clinging to Anglicanism for the sake of the lovely and gracious things in its past, you are likely to be disillusioned before long. We are in for a difficult and muddling time. Unless you can believe in the C. of E. for the sake of what it *is* in itself and for the sake of its place in God's intention for His Church, I don't think you can possibly ever be either very happy or very secure as an Anglican in the next few years. I entirely agree with what you say, that you 'feel you must be a Catholic first of all'. Of course! But if that means that we have to be 'Anglicans afterwards' or only with hyphens or apologies, then it means that we cannot be Anglicans at all. Unless we are 'Catholics' inasmuch as and *because* we are 'Anglicans', then we are not being 'Catholics'. Unless you believe that an Anglican is *as such* a fully living 'member' of the 'Body of Christ' – unless you believe that, not only emotionally but rationally, for intelligent and intelligible reasons, I don't think a man of your intelligence and awareness will be able to 'live to God' *as* an Anglican for very long – *i.e.* you won't be able, even as a layman, to go on steadily and quietly leading your spiritual life without being distracted and unsettled by shocks and controversies. The laity can as a rule leave these things aside to a considerable extent: they are remote from the worship and prayer and the moral endeavour to lead a good Christian life, which between them form the main *interest* of religion for the ordinary layman. But certain big clashes and strains seem to be unavoidable now in the position into which the C. of E. has allowed itself to drift. No educated or keen churchman will be able altogether to ignore them in the form they are taking. On the other hand, if you do believe in the C. of E., the kind of thing which is happening now about this S. Indian business will sometimes make your belief in it seem very academic and your hopes for it very unreal. But I don't think it will make them seem *untrue*.

I do think that the sort of intelligent belief in the C. of E. I am trying to indicate is necessary nowadays; and yet that it can be combined with the sort of living discontent with things as they are now in the C. of E. which things as they are now certainly warrant. What we have to avoid is sinking into that sterile and embittered contempt for Anglican authority in its own legitimate field, and for 'the Bishops', which did so much to frustrate the old 'Anglo-Catholic Party' of the 1920's. It really did harm to their own souls . . .

I think I do believe in Anglicanism that way – anyhow, I hope I do. That is why I wonder whether I am the right person to 'help' you in the way you ask just now. I don't particularly want to send you the sort of cut-and-dried 'answer' to O'D.'s type-script for which you ask, because I don't really believe that sort of way of dealing with things can ever ultimately 'help' anybody very much. I agree that the technical question about Anglican Orders must be an essential preliminary to any such belief in the C. of E. And from the technical point of view there *is* an answer to each one of O'D.'s points. (None of them are new – he is using a manual, supplemented by Messenger's book on *The Reformation, the Mass and the Priesthood*.) But the historical evidence is in some way a tangled business for both sides. O'D. and I could probably exchange brickbats about Cardinal Pole[1] and Bishop Gordon[2] 'across you' by letter for weeks or months, without either of us really 'helping' at all. If I were to try to do anything, I would much rather try to put the case 'constructively' than 'defensively', so to speak, and to leave you with materials for forming your own judgement. You would quite likely wonder what on earth some of them had to do with the question. But in the end I think you would probably get a clearer view of the real issues. It would be more trouble for you – and involve a lot more writing for me! And I dare say you are far too busy now at the Board of Trade preventing us all having things, to deal with it in that way. If you say so, I shall quite understand.

I ought to add – Don't think I am pretending to be impartial about this question! I do see that what is at issue in this particular controversy with Rome about our Orders is a *sine qua non*, the essential foundation, for any idea of Anglicanism worth an intelligent man's holding in these days, when 'the fountains of the great deep are broken up'. I should try to put before you a case for one side, an advocate's case, though as fairly as a man can who has come to a decided judgement on a disputed issue. But I don't believe that the real reasons for being an Anglican *begin* with that. They begin after that has been settled. I don't particularly object to controversy and argument about this sort of issue. But I fear that we clergy often behave rather badly and unfairly to the laity in dragging them into this sort of technical question, and I suspect they are mostly either bored or bewildered by it. Clerics are usually rather argumentative people anyhow, and these things have a 'professional' interest and importance for us. Perhaps that makes our conduct in inflicting them on you at least human, if it does not quite excuse it. We enjoy talking our particular kind of 'shop', like most men. But we ought to remember that it is 'shop'.

Let me know what you want. I promise to try to be intelligible, at all events. But if you dislike the prospect of reading technical stuff, or if you are too busy, you needn't be afraid to say so. Yrs. Ever *in Dño*, Gr. D.

(QAO 7–11)


18. iii. '44


My dear Harry, Thank you for your letter – and thank you for your thanks. But I was glad to have the chance of doing it since you wanted it, and anyhow it is part of my job. As for O'Dwyer's letter, I am sure that in fairness you ought to see him again since he says he wants to see you, and you ought to listen to anything he says with an open mind. I have said all along that what I was giving you was an advocate's case, and that I should leave you to make your own judgement at the end. You can show him anything I have sent you, and I shall be grateful for any corrections of fact or other criticisms he cares to make, either directly to me or through you.

But whether you see him or not, remember that I have only been putting before you what I regard as reasons why Anglicans have not that sort of obvious and imperative duty to leave the Church of England which *Apostolicae Curae*[3] would imply, if it were true. If the C. of E. has valid Orders and Sacraments then it is *possible* to be an Anglican. But whether it is *right* to be an Anglican would depend on other considerations. As I said before, the positive reasons for being an Anglican begin only after that point is settled. I think there are such reasons – godly and weighty reasons (No! Don't be alarmed! I am not going to start all over again about a fresh subject) but we have hardly touched on them here at all. Only I don't want you to get the idea that belief in the C. of E. only means escaping on a sort of 'Not proven' verdict from the particular charges brought by Leo XIII, to resume a slightly shady career on the fringes of decent ecclesiastical society. As I also said before, only those who believe in the C. of E. as a genuine and living part of the Holy Catholic Church are likely to be able to lead their spiritual life securely and steadily within her in the next few years. Without that belief, based on genuine and informed conviction, you will find yourself too much harassed and distracted by the continual controversies and upsets which it seems to me are inescapable in the very complicated situation which has slowly been growing up in the C. of E. for the last generation and more. The causes of it are intricate and many go back a long way. And the situation has got worse by degrees, through the adoption of a policy of always trying to avoid deciding any practical issue on grounds of doctrinal belief. That is always a dangerous and doubtful policy for any Christian to adopt, let alone a Church. (It can easily become immoral.) But it was adopted *faute de mieux* in the C. of E. – not merely because it saved trouble, but because in the circumstances of State Establishment any other policy was hardly a practicable possibility. But now that the accumulated consequences are working themselves out, we cannot expect that they will be comfortable or trivial.

It was by your own showing some inkling of all this which first upset you last year, and if you see Father O'Dwyer he is quite entitled to face you with it. Indeed, I think that if I were a Roman controversialist I should stop looking for the Achilles' heel in the Anglican *Ordinal*, and concentrate all my arguments on the shyness of official Anglicanism of *acting like* a Catholic Church. (I don't mean in ceremonial things and trifles, but on doctrinal issues and principles of the first importance.) It is very apt in practice to reserve its Catholic beliefs solely as something to point to in self-defence against Roman Catholic controversy, and to trust to a purely opportunist policy and a rather ramshackle institutionalism to guide the actual life of the Church. As a rule Roman Catholic controversialists let themselves be hypnotised by *Apostolicae Curae* and pay attention only to that. It is natural, because it settles the question for them – and it is a 'short cut' (and was meant to be). But like so many short cuts it only increases difficulties for those who take it.

But if O'Dwyer takes the other line, it is a fair one to take, and you ought to consider it. I think that the real answer lies in the circumstances of the Reformation in England. When the Elizabethan government presented the Church of England with a *fait accompli* by simply imposing the third Act of Uniformity through Parliament in 1559 without even a pretence of consultation with the Church, there were two possible lines to be taken. – One was covert and unorganised refusal to accept the situation, which meant utter disruption. The government was in complete control of all the machinery of the Church. You have only to study the confusion and disorganisation of the Recusants in Elizabeth's reign to see the consequences of this if it had been generally adopted. It would have meant the end of organised Christianity in England in a welter of disintegration. The other was the attempt to work *through* the situation, if the essentials were there, and to do the best one could with those. The Recusants adopted the one course of action, and heroically endured the consequences. But I do not think that honest and devoted men like Archbishop Parker[4] and Bishop Guest[5] were to be blamed if they thought the other was the more constructively Christian line to take. Perhaps that was the first of our dangerous decisions by 'policy'. Yet there was much in the legacy of the Mediaeval Church which cried aloud for Reform. Politics – in certain respects very grubby politics – complicated the whole question. Neither Philip of Spain on one side nor Cecil and Leicester on the other are very attractive Christian protagonists, you know. Nor were either Elizabeth or Mary Queen of Scots, the Protestant and Catholic candidates for the throne, looking solely to the spiritual profit of the causes they represented. And so the breach widened and deepened and hardened on both sides, and the blood of martyrs did not do anything to heal it. The two Churches developed very differently, largely through the fact of their separation. But the question really is, *were* the essentials there in the system which Parker and Guest and the others felt obliged to accept? That is a much wider question than Anglican Orders, and I am not going into it now. But I cannot see that they were not. And if they were, then for three centuries the C. of E. taught the essentials of the Catholic Faith and ministered the essential Catholic Sacraments to the ordinary English people, when no one else could, or would have been allowed by the State to do it. That is her title to exist, and I think a man could and should love her for that, even if he felt that he must leave her now, because it did not seem to him a title to an *independent* existence to-day.

You may say that the position is not quite the same now. There are proposals – you know of them and we need not go into them – by which that Catholic Faith and those Catholic Sacraments are not repudiated by the Church of England, but by which they are treated, for the first time in our history, as something 'optional'. It is suggested that those who do not believe in them and do not want them could contract out of them, to a greater or lesser extent, if they were disposed to come to some working arrangement with the machinery of the Church of England without them. The idea is that we should just treat them as things we want to keep for ourselves, but not as in any sense integral parts of the Christian revelation. The men who have planned this have hoped and prayed all their lives for Reunion.

And Reunion with Rome is difficult, and the difficulties are not all on our side. So they have chosen the easy way (and another 'short cut'). Old men in a hurry to realise their dearest dreams can be very short-sighted. Though for a while it might not be admitted, Anglicanism would quietly have changed its position on all the fundamental questions which divide Catholicism from Protestantism. The Anglican Church and Ministry would have been equated with various Protestant societies and Ministries as slightly variant specimens of the same thing, by the process of ignoring all those differences which revolve around the idea of 'Justification' with their immense effects on every aspect of the *living* of the Christian life. At present Anglicanism and Protestantism stand on opposite sides of this great division of thought. But if these dreams came true, the stand first taken up in the 39 *Articles* and maintained ever since by the C. of E. would be bound to be reversed in the end. To take one instance out of many: You could not convincingly teach, as our Catechism now does, that Baptism is 'generally (*i.e.* universally) *necessary to salvation*', if you were not prepared to insist on it as necessary for receiving Holy Communion or even Ordination – as these proposals deliberately omit to insist on it. As regards the question of Orders, what these proposals amount to is an official Anglican admission that Pope Leo XIII was right after all in his fundamental contention in *Apostolicae Curae*. In spite of face-saving phrases about 'the Apostolic Ministry' and the future confining of the act of Ordaining to men styled 'Bishops', we should be committed to a formal declaration that by 'Bishops, Priests and Deacons' *could* be meant only the new sixteenth-century conception of the Ministry disguised under the old titles, and that anyone who chose to take it as meaning that would be fully justified in doing so. And whether we like it or not, that would be to justify Leo XIII in the teeth of all our own past history. Thus, if these proposals were to be put into practice, the whole ground for believing in the Church of England which I have outlined would have ceased to exist – within the Church of England thus revolutionised. Nevertheless, as regards *the past* the facts we have been considering would not therefore cease to be *true*. But those who accepted their truth would have to face the unhappy situation that there was no longer any legitimate place for them in the new Church of England, or in the Church of Rome either.

I said before that conditional loyalties weary a man's heart in the end. With a quite undesigned cruelty it is just such a conditional loyalty to the Church of England as she is which has been forced just now upon those who believe in the Church of England for what she is. I should be less than candid if I did not tell you that, not because you are going to see O'Dwyer, but because it is the fact. He does not believe in the C. of E. and therefore he can hardly understand or put before you this desperate unhappiness that only an Anglican can feel. I think some of us would never be altogether happy again if what these good and sincere men hope for in South India and elsewhere were to come to pass. We should have a choice of wilderness in which to serve the Lord – and that would be about all.

I have been candid, because I know – nobody better – that it is a difficult loyalty in these days that I have put before you. But is it more difficult to hold it sincerely than to accept sincerely the statements I put before you at the end of my last letter? (We need pass no hard judgements on Roman Catholics for holding to them. They have no need to analyse them or to do more than take the Bull for granted. It is otherwise with us.) This may not seem a very cheerful or triumphant conclusion. Yet for myself I find that our Lord is good to attempts to see the truth and follow it. But you will choose for yourself with the help that He gives you. Remember me to Father O'Dwyer if you see him. Yours ever *in Dño.* Gr. D.

(*QAO* 84–9)

## Notes

1. Reginald Pole (1500–58) was Archbishop of Canterbury (1556–8) in the reign of Queen Mary.

2. John Gordon was consecrated Bishop of Galloway in 1688. He was received into the Roman Catholic Church in 1704 and, after an investigation, Pope Clement XI declared his Anglican orders invalid.

3. The Papal Bull issued by Leo XIII in 1896 declaring Anglican orders 'absolutely null and utterly void'.

4. Matthew Parker (1504–75) was Archbishop of Canterbury from 1559 until his death in 1575.

5. Edmund Guest (1514–77) was consecrated Bishop of Rochester in 1560 and translated to Salisbury in 1571.

## Catholicism Today

*On 31 October 1949 The Times published an article by an unnamed special correspondent under the title: 'Catholicism To-day: Relations between Rome and the Christian World'. Calling for 'free and open discussion with qualified representatives of the various Christian bodies', it touched a raw ecclesiastical nerve which unleashed a torrent of correspondence. Although Dix's name was cited in two of these letters, he himself did not contribute to the debate at the time, preferring to wait until the following article, divided between two editions of the weekly non-party journal* Time and Tide, *was published in February of the following year.*

Educated Englishmen used to relish an ecclesiastical dogfight above most forms of sport, probably because English clerics of all brands are apt on their own topics to puncture each other with a special sort of refined but zestful and dexterous unkindness, very agreeable for well-read spectators. That the taste for such bouts is not dead was evident from the exceptional attention evoked by a *Times* article from a Special Correspondent on "Catholicism Today" published on 31 October, and the unusually lengthy and distinguished correspondence which followed.

The letters mostly displayed an urbanity unprecedented in such exchanges: dissident Christians seem to be learning courtesy just when standards of secular controversy everywhere are reaching unheard-of depths of vulgarity and vituperative clumsiness. This high level was partly due to a wise and opportune letter from Dom Columba Cary-Elwes, of Ampleforth, matched by a reply from the Dean of Winchester.[1] They saved the subject just when the traditional Catholic-Protestant rumpus seemed about to start. But chiefly it was due to the serenity of the original article, whose high concern with something far above casual polemics could not be mistaken. The writer dealt with a subject serious indeed for his fellow-Catholics in England, but equally serious for the future of all English religion, and of all English "culture" in the widest sense. (That is a moderate estimate of its importance. The implications reach much farther than that.)

The republication in pamphlet form of the article, correspondence and concluding *Times* leader, makes clear in retrospect what was subtly indicated by the Special Correspondent but only intermittently

visible in the thick of the subsequent letters, that this time the core of
the discussion was not an old-fashioned row between Papalists and
Protestants. It was a discreet though lively exchange of views between
two sets of devoted Roman Catholics on the question of what relations, if any, a good Catholic can have with his fellow-Christians
outside the Roman Communion *quâ* Christians. (This is a general
question, touching Catholics everywhere, but it was discussed chiefly
in terms of the English situation.)

This domestic discussion had to be carried on amid distracting
incursions from Anglicans, about the basis of the Petrine claims and
the freedom of St Mary from original sin, which naturally were repelled with an equally distracting vigour. (It is odd that we Anglicans always seem to get so much more excited about these somewhat
peripheral doctrines than about the whole contents of the Apostles'
Creed on which we agree with the Pope.) This led, for old times'
sake, to some interchange of well-worn brickbats about the validity
of Anglican Orders. But all these were irrelevances. Free Churchmen,
whether imitating Gallio or Gamaliel, made no significant interven-
tion. The essential issue – raised only, not settled – was, what exactly
do Roman Catholics mean by "the Catholic Church"?

That may sound a foolish and provocative thing to say, about
Roman Catholics of all people. They have an immediate and clear
answer to that question: "All baptised Christians in communion
with the Pope". Setting aside refinements, here irrelevant, about
things like "invincible ignorance" and the "Mystical Body", all the
Roman Catholics who took part in the debate would undoubtedly
have agreed in returning that answer.

But the simple formula covers the possibility of considerable practical divergence, according to whether you place the greater emphasis
on "baptised Christians" or on "communion with the Pope". It is
theoretically possible to lay an equal emphasis on each, but in practice impossible, because there are unfortunately hundreds of millions
of "baptised Christians" who for various reasons are not "in communion with the Pope". If these are to be altogether excluded from
what you mean by "the Catholic Church", baptism is in fact subordi-
nated to Papal Communion as the test of membership. It seems fair
to say that Catholic theology has always laid greater emphasis on
baptism, but the ecclesiastical practice has for some centuries tended
to lay more emphasis on Papal Communion as the test – naturally,
since it was the latter which was denied.

At all events, *The Times* correspondence manifested a distinct divergence, at least of emphasis, on this point among English Roman Catholics, with the possibility of important practical consequences, depending upon which view was adopted. This is not to suggest that any tendency to "doctrinal compromise" appeared among any Roman Catholics. It did not. It was the practical consequences which were in debate, but they depend on a theological divergence. It seems to have been the intention of the Special Correspondent to bring this divergence into the open in the most public fashion possible (hence the choice of *The Times* instead of some Catholic publication) with a special eye to those possible consequences.

But why should a theological difference among Roman Catholics about the theoretical limits of "the Catholic Church" be of much importance to the rest of us – above all in England, where they form a small minority, some 5 per cent of the population? The reasons are far-reaching, complex and manifold. Here are a selection:

The West is slowly drawing together to face the most tremendous menace to all that has been meant by "Christendom" since Charles Martel repelled the Saracens at Tours in the eighth century. Among innumerable other things, Christendom includes all that European men have come to understand by the worth and freedom of the individual. This "Liberal" estimate of man does not make much sense apart from its Christian roots and presuppositions, though the "Liberals" mostly ignored that in their palmy days. It is only because men and women go to heaven or hell for all eternity and States and institutions do not, that each man and woman *can* be recognised to have an inviolable significance, over against what is from the purely material and historical standpoint the enormously more important human fact of society. Only if the individual is also an "immortal soul", uniquely precious as such to a God who is the foundation of all existence, can you attribute to him in all circumstances indefeasible human rights against the State. The Western view of man is essentially a spiritual view of man, dependent on belief in God, and in particular on the Christian doctrine of God. That is now threatened by an attempt to organise life by the logical consequences of a *doctrine* of Atheism, involving a materialistic view of man.

That is why the West is rallying round the Christians. Not that the West now contains anything like a majority of *convinced* Christians of any kind (*i.e.* of people who believe Christian dogma and, therefore, regularly worship in Church, and try outside Church to live consistently with their beliefs). The Western idea of man would be in much less imminent danger if it were not menaced within the

West itself by the quick decay of so many other inheritances from "Christendom" among its largely post-Christian populations. But all really radical human differences are about the meaning of human life – that is, they are at bottom theological, inevitably. And so the Christians are at the heart of the Western rally. The Politburo are not fools; nor was Hitler. They have a creed and a dogma and an idol of their own. And so it is the *worshipping* Christians they worry about. The rest are makeweights, from their point of view. They are quite right. If we may trust Holy Scripture, and if real life means what it seems to mean, God – and the devil also – are of the same opinion. It is in worship that belief comes to its point in life.

Unmistakably, with the resurgence of Christendom, Rome is becoming again the heart of the West. At a time when France, Free Germany, Italy, Belgium, Switzerland, Austria, Spain, Portugal, Eire (who expected it thirty years ago?) all have practising Catholic premiers, each chosen partly because he is known to be a Catholic, Rome in England counts nationally for little. And Britain, which is preponderantly England, is as necessary to the West, of which it is an inseparable part, as the West is to Britain. Otherwise the spiritual view of man is not likely to be effectually defended. And Britain, beyond a vague uneasiness, shows very little awareness of what is involved.

Religion largely fails to provide a framework for English thinking or English life. The broad result of the last 400 years of our religious history has been to set up three different main types of worship and doctrine (Roman, Anglican and Puritan) each now possessing strong roots in the past, with an outlook and pieties and prejudices, and to some extent a social "sub-culture", unshared by the other two. They are roughly equal in numbers – rather more than 2,000,000 each – 20 per cent of the population taken together. (That seems about the proportion of *worshipping* Christians in other Western countries, except in specially devout regions.) There is no prospect that any of them will absorb the others *en bloc*. The existence of the other two hinders each from converting any large proportion of the unattached 80 per cent, which is becoming progressively de-Christianised without knowing it.

It was this disturbing situation, in its ecumenical aspects, but with particular reference to the situation religious and national in England, which *The Times* article analysed from the standpoint of a loyal Roman Catholic but with a realism that flattered his fellow-Catholics not at all. That unsparing picture evidently shook the noticeable self-complacency of English Romanism. There have been deprecations and some indignation in Catholic periodicals, but singularly few challenges to its general accuracy. What the author emphasised was the urgent need for collaboration among Christians. What he indicated, delicately but firmly, was that this will certainly involve doctrinal discussion and mutual explanation between separated Christians, of an unprecedentedly dispassionate kind; and why it is that, perhaps for the first time since the Reformation, the theological situation among Christians (quite apart from external pressures) might offer some prospects for such discussions. What he did not say or even imply, but what is true, is that if the English Roman Catholics played their part patiently and wisely in such undertakings, they might soon find themselves leading their fellow-Christians and many others of their countrymen (as they do now in Germany and France) as they have not been able to do in England since the Catholic Lord Howard defeated the Armada. And this time the cause would not be only national, but Christian.

This raises at once the question of what sort of relations are possible for the loyal Catholic with other baptised Christians, and that depends on how you define membership of "the Catholic Church".

Co-operation of separated Christians in England is particularly difficult because of the "triangular" relationship between Roman Catholics, Anglicans and Free Churchmen, which has no exact parallel elsewhere. Under the leadership of Cardinal Hinsley and Archbishop Temple this difficulty was surmounted on certain great national problems; since then it has rather languished. Collaboration between Anglicans and Free Churchmen has survived, but its products have been distinctly less impressive. At bottom this is, no doubt, a question of leadership. And even in this reduced form it has not always been easy and has sometimes broken down. On purely social questions it has occasionally been effective (*e.g.* on the sale of contraceptives from slot machines). But there are very few purely social questions. Whenever questions arise on which Christian religious insight might give a different answer from the conventional ethic of the day, the leadership tends to be fumbling and the pronouncements to be hesitant and platitudinous. This is partly because Anglican and (especially) Free Church leaders cannot speak with much authority for their followers without lengthy (and usually impracticable) constitutional procedure; partly, I fear it must be said, because both are theologically very divided and doctrinally weak in adherence to principles. The former is more cripplingly true of Anglicanism, the latter probably of Free Churchmen.

In what is becoming known, not very prettily or accurately, as "Home Evangelism", though the un-churched public professes to be repelled by sectarian differences, experience seems to show that joint efforts are in the long run less effectual than well-organised "missions" by one body alone. (Thus, *e.g.*, the recent "Mission to London" of the Church of England scored a modest but distinct success compared with the united "Christian Commando Campaign" – though the latter was probably handicapped by its preposterous name.) This is natural. "Evangelism" is from all points of view frustrated unless it eventually leads the converts on to a life of righteousness in the worshipping Church. That is the consummation of conversion. This is less likely to be achieved if the Joint Evangelists can only present their converts with competing consummations of their Joint Evangelsim.

On the whole, cordial as many of the efforts to make it successful have been, collaboration between Anglicans and Free Churchmen has been disappointing in its "National impact". It has often led to better understanding between the participants, and that eventually may be an important gain. But the British public has so far had some reason not to be much impressed. Is there any reason to think that turning this difficult relation *à deux* into a triangle by importing Roman Catholics would have a good effect?

Obviously many on both sides thought it could serve no useful purpose. The Auxiliary Bishop of Brentwood[2] made himself the chief spokesman of this standpoint and, though his letter gave some offence by a certain pointedness, it is just to observe that he had evidently had much more practical experience of the attempts to arrive at such collaboration on national and social issues under Cardinal Hinsley[3] and Archbishop Temple[4] than any other correspondent. The long list he gave of matters on which it had in fact proved impossible to produce a common statement or take common action was dismaying. It has to be remembered that Catholicism is not only a system of theology and worship. It is also a philosophy, an ethic, a way of life, all of which in the minds of its adherents hang together, and which among them offer plentiful opportunities of difference from those who do not share the Catholic presuppositions in some of these fields. Thus, *e.g.* Catholicism takes with the utmost seriousness the teaching of Jesus that the remarriage of divorced persons is simply "adultery". Though others may suspect them, rightly or wrongly, of sometimes opening a back-door by over-easy "Decrees of Nullity", they are adamant on the principle that there can be no dissolution in the eyes of God of any valid marriage except by the death of one of the partners. Protestants, on the other hand, and some members of the Church of England seem increasingly (and surprisingly) willing to revise the plain words of Christ on this matter (Mt. 19.9; Lk. 16.18) and to accept the standards of the contemporary world as a guide in their place. Here, to give but one instance, is a whole class of social questions on which common pronouncements would be exceedingly difficult.

From the Anglican side, however, the Bishop of Winchester[5] raised a primary difficulty about any such collaboration by other baptised Christians with Roman Catholics in this country. It is that, apparently under the direction of their bishops, Roman Catholics have great hesitation in praying together with other Christians. Difficulties have been raised about saying the Lord's Prayer together, or even praying silently in one another's company. As the Bishop of Winchester said, Christian cooperation (and it is that, as such, which is in question) which excludes *any* sort of prayer to and with the same Lord together, "feels in experience to be frozen at the start".

To this Bishop Beck replied that:

United Prayer, if it is to mean anything at all, must be an expression of united minds. But a Catholic and a non-Catholic saying the Lord's Prayer could not have united minds or mean the same thing. The Catholic saying, *e.g.* "Thy kingdom come" would be praying for the conversion of all men to Catholicism; the non-Catholic evidently would not subscribe to this petition. It would pain the Bishop of Winchester that Catholics should be dubious about his giving a blessing at a joint meeting. But their attitude is the logical outcome of their belief that, so far as they are concerned and from their point of view, the Bishop of Winchester is a layman. Surely it is better in all these matters to be quite frank . . .

Is "frankness" quite the right description of this? It rather looks as though the Auxiliary Bishop of Brentwood was pulling his punches a little, out of sheer consideration for the Bishop of Winchester's feelings. With great respect, this is the sort of nonsense we all talk when we try to substitute sentiment for theology. The introduction of the question of Anglican Orders at this point, though admittedly tempting, is unfortunate because it confuses Bishop Beck's main point, about united prayer requiring united minds. There is nothing whatever in the Lord's Prayer which makes it unsuitable for use in the presence of a layman (or indeed of any theist, one might have thought). But Bishop Beck does not quite regard the Bishop of Winchester as having the status of a Roman Catholic "layman". That is the whole trouble. He regards him as a *schismatic* layman, having ecclesiastical authority from an illegitimate society of Christians, and apparently of so heretical a turn that the very words of the Lord's Prayer are bound to take on in his mind a meaning that no traditional Christian could possibly subscribe to. As for laymen and blessings, I suppose that Catholic fathers have sometimes blessed their sons and also the family meals; and Solomon, if I remember rightly, was of the opinion that "by the blessing of the upright the city is exalted" without apparently considering the question of Holy Orders. No one is committed to any belief about anyone's clerical status by a blessing.

But let us return to the Lord's Prayer, Bishop Beck's main point. Catholics do, as a matter of fact mean a great deal more by "Thy kingdom come" than just "the conversion of all men to Catholicism". If every man, woman and child in the world had been baptised into the Papal Communion, there would be even greater need than now to pray "Thy kingdom come". There is always sin. And the Christians would be distressingly secure, and it is always when we feel secure that we forget in dozens of ways (including ecclesiastical presumption) that "*Thine* is the kingdom . . . "

When two men pray "Thy kingdom come" one of them may have (usually does have) a greater understanding of what the words involve. But if they are *praying*, neither can hope to impose his own limited interpretation on God. Both are seeking to impose *all* that it means, whatever it means, on their own rebellious wills. That is how Catholics pray the Lord's Prayer – and so do other Christians. Does Christian baptism and faith in God and Christ make no difference whatever to a man outside the communion of the Pope? It was Pope St Stephen in the third century who vindicated the truth that even received outside the Church, it meant incorporation into Christ and could not be repeated. If the Body of Christ and "the Catholic Church" are not in some sense co-extensive, then all Catholic Ecclesiology since St Paul has been grievously misleading.

It is not surprising to find Roman Catholics in some disagreement on this topic. It is the sore point of all twentieth century Christian thinking, the point where all problems run together for Protestants and Catholics alike, though not in precisely the same way. There is a great nostalgia for unity and without Rome as the centre and head unity is impossible.

But the Holy See is hesitating how to act in an unprecedented situation and is at the moment merely repeating traditional gestures, with occasional friendly smiles interspersed. Meanwhile its adherents in England accept with an astonishing complacency the position of a people apart, largely unintelligible to their fellow-countrymen; more than one of their clergy has explained to me that it is to this they owe their "immense prestige". "Prestige" they have, but they owe it to their treasures of ordered thought and heroic faithfulness to certain gospel insights, which other Christians badly need. They are frightened of being thought willing to "compromise". To anyone with an inkling of history the Papacy must in any case appear the most august institution on earth. It was thundering its theocratic claims across the world before the Caesars fell, before any of the modern States were born. It has never flinched from their consequences in all the disasters of its most eventful history. It is strange that its English adherents can suppose that we shall forget all that unless they are allowed to recite the Penny Catechism to us every time we meet. Even where she lets herself go slatternly, the Roman Church is usually *très grande dame*. It is only in England that she sinks to this curious nervous protestation of her own gentility.

The question is not of the Papacy, which is a vast Christian fact. It is a question of the Papacy's relation to "the Catholic Church", a still vaster fact – about which Roman Catholics have still to make up their own minds in some important ways.

Surveying the Correspondence, I think that if I were a Free Churchman I should ponder on the fact that when a great religious and national question was discussed no Free Churchman made any contribution. "Where there is no vision the people perish." If I were a Roman Catholic I think I might make a self-examination on both halves of the Petrine text, "and when thou art converted – strengthen thy brethren". Being an established Anglican, I shall make my self-examination on various uncomfortable aspects of "No man can serve two masters."

(*Time and Tide*, 4 February 1950, 107–8;
11 February 1950, 131–2)

## Notes

1. Edward Selwyn (1885–1959).
2. George Beck (1904–78) was translated to Salford in 1955 and became Archbishop of Liverpool in 1964.

3. Arthur Hinsley (1865–1943) became Archbishop of Westminster in 1935.
4. William Temple (1881–1944) became Archbishop of Canterbury in 1942.
5. Mervyn Haigh (1887–1962) was Bishop of Winchester from 1942 to 1952.

## Letters to Mother

*The following letters, written by Dix to his mother just before his clothing as a novice in 1936, provide a fascinating insight into his commitment to the work of reunion with Rome.*

23 September 1936

My darling Mother,

I was to have been clothed as a Novice on the evening of the 13th, but it has had to be put off for a rather wonderful though very frightening reason. While I was away, Father Abbot received from France a number of invitations for me to go across and lecture on the English Church and Reunion. I start on Saturday for Lyons. I am lecturing there on Monday and Tuesday to clergy and laity and speaking at the Grand Seminaire and the Jesuit College. On Tuesday morning I hope to go to Ars to make a pilgrimage to the shrine of the saints, Saint Jean Marie Vianney (who prophesied the Reunion of the Church of England and Rome) and where a special mass is said every week for Nashdom. Tuesday night I shall spend at Notre-Dame des Dombes, a Trappist Monastery with whom we have friendly relations and mutual prayers for Unity. Wednesday, I go to Paray-le-Monial on pilgrimage to the Church in which our Lord revealed the devotion to the Sacred Heart to Saint Margaret Marie Alacoque, to her shrine and that of Blessed Claude de la Colombière, and to have a conference with some Jesuit theologians at their Maison de la Colombière. Sunday afternoon, I believe, I am to visit Cardinal Maurin the Archbishop. Thursday, I go to Paris to stay with the Superior of Saint Sulpice and conference with the professors. Friday morning, with the Dominicans at Juvisy; Friday evening a public lecture at the Action Populaire to clergé. Saturday, I am to see Cardinal Verdier the Archbishop of Paris, and Saturday evening, back home. With luck, I shall enter the Novitiate Sunday evening October 14th.

It is a wonderful thing, because the initiative has come entirely from the French side, not from us! The visit, of course, is entirely unofficial. There is no question of "negotiations" or ANYTHING formal like that. But it is still the day of small things. The more these unofficial contacts can be increased, the more the desire for Union will grow and the more PRAYERS for unity will multiply, and that CANNOT fail in the end. But you must pray and pray very hard for me while I am away. I shall need it very much. Pray that I may be ABSOLUTELY obedient to grace, that I may do all that our Lord wants me to do in France, and try to do nothing else. It is the sort of occasion on which one can do INCALCULABLE harm by getting carried away and minimising differences and difficulties in the way of DOGMATIC agreement, which is the only "unity" worth considering. If you should be that way, ask the prayers of the Sisters at Filsham Road. I am immensely humbled that our Lord should have given me this to do, and very frightened of spoiling it.

As soon as I get back, I shall be going into Retreat for a week, and then, I shall have to get down to proofs of my book. But I will let you know how things go.

All my love, Darling, and pray for me. Go to mass for me if you can manage, and offer it for me while I am away. It will be such a safeguard and comfort to know you are doing it.

Your ALSTON

4 October 1936

My darling Mother,

I will make this as much of a screed as I can, but I have only four hours for twenty-three letters accumulated while I was away. Tonight, I enter the Novitiate and go into retreat for ten days.

The French trip was wonderful, and I know it is due to the prayers of those in England. We went to Paris on the Friday night and on to Lyon Saturday a.m. after hearing mass at Saint Antione. We were met at Lyon by the Abbé Couturier, sent by the Archbishop to meet us. On Sunday, we heard a mass at the Adoration Reparatrice, a special mass for unity, and there were carried off to the Convents of Jesus Marie, the Cenacle and the Visitation, and to see the Basilica of Notre Dame de Fouvières. Frightful! Exactly like trying to pray in the Albert Memorial! But, enormous and full of people. Then, we prayed for a long time in the little chapel where Saint Thomas à Becket used to say mass in exile. Then, we went to the Lazarists to meet some theologians for a discussion and, after that, to the Cathedral, and then to Saint Martin d'Ainay for Vespers, followed by dinner and a lecture to clergy. Monday, we were taken to the Trappists of Notre-Dame des Dombes. Quite wonderful! In the afternoon, we made a pilgrimage in a car driven by a Jesuit novice to Ars, where we prayed for about two hours at the shrine. The Curé d'Ars prophesied 80 years ago the reunion of Canterbury and Rome, when it seemed impossible! In the evening another lecture to clergé. Tuesday a.m. mass at the Adoration Reparatrice for unity, followed by a visit to the Russian church and more prayers for unity – Romans, Orthodox and Anglican priests praying in turn round the altar, and then giving the kiss of peace all round. Wonderfully moving! Then, on to see the Chancellor at the Archbishop's Palace. The Cardinal was away. But he had left a whole paper of questions! We did the best we could with these and then had a long talk with Mgr. Bechetoile. Afternoon, a big conference to professors of the Faculté Catholique. Jesuits and Lazarists and some secular clergé. Two and three-quarter hours and they were still interested! Tuesday evening, back to Paris and a mild railway accident, getting in only at 3.30am instead of 11. We were met by the Abbé Dumontet, Directeur of Saint Sulpice. The next morning, Mass at Saint Sulpice, followed by a terrific lunch at the Séminaire des Carmes (five wines, seven courses, sweet champagne and speeches! followed by the most revolting liquor I have ever tasted!) followed by a conference to the heads of all the seminaries in Paris and the Archbishop's secretary. Not too easy, because I had left my notes at Lyon. However, they arrived next morning, and everybody seemed to grasp what I was getting at. Many questions, and obviously intense interest. Then to the Séminaire Saint Sulpice (600 students). Dinner at High Table with the professors and visit to Chapel for Prières du Soir, where they put us in choir next to Superior General! Then, a visit from the editor of the *Révue Apologetique*.

The next morning, to Juisvy to the Dominicans; lunch, conference and discussion. 5.30pm the Cardinal. He had arranged to give us ten minutes. He kept us forty, asking innumerable questions and finally impounded my lecture notes which, he said, he MUST have! He said: "Working on these lines, you will surely achieve unity. It will certainly come. But, we must not be in any hurry. It is still a generation away; there is an immense work to be done in both churches to implant the DESIRE for union. With that, we can do everything. Even you may not live to see it, though you are still young. ('Oh! la jeunesse, la jeunesse!') I shall not see it, though I shall have helped to prepare it. But, you MUST continue as you are doing, by prayer, above all, and by personal contacts. Multiply these, and it cannot fail." At the end, he said: "I go tomorrow (Friday) to say the monthly mass of the Sacred Heart at Montmartre for France. But I will say it instead for YOU, for all your intentions, for your work for unity, for your monastery, for your friends, for ALL your intentions", and he gave us his blessing and asked OUR prayers. You may be sure I took care to put in you and Ron and Eileen and all here into the Canon while I heard his mass next morning.

On the Friday, we went to the Jesuits of the Action Populaire, then, on to the Jesuits of the Maison des Études, after lunch at the Action Populaire, where we met the Provincial of Paris. He was charming! We went to Chapel with them after lunch for "Recollection" and, again, they put us beside the Superior. Then, for half an hour, to see the Head of the Jeunesse Catholique Française, who will circulate 200,000 (!) leaflets among their members for the Church Unity Octave. Then, rush for the train and the night boat. A fearfully crowded week! But we have secured that the French Church will officially keep the Octave next year, and the Cardinals of Paris and Lyon will each preside officially in their cathedrals. So also will the Bishop elect of Nantes, whom we met at Saint Sulpice. The Jesuits and Dominicans, who generally squabble a lot, are equally enthusiastic and are each supplying preachers for it. I had a warm invitation to go to several other places, but simply could not fit in. But those who invited us seemed delighted with the results achieved and the interest aroused.

Will you tell them at the Convent that I went for a little while into what, I was told, was the old Couvent des Oiseaux, (now a "ministry" of sorts) and said a "Salve Regina" to our Lady of Victories for the return of the Cononesses; there was no time for more. Also, I met a Jesuit who knew Monsieur le Chanoine Guillaume.

It has been wonderful! Now, I have returned to an immense accumulation of work, which will grow worse during the retreat. I am so glad you will be able to teach at the Convent. No time for more. All my love. Will write after retreat.

ALSTON

## Letters to Frederick Green

*Frederick Green was Chaplain of Merton College, Oxford, when Dix was an undergraduate, and from there went on to be Vice-Dean of Norwich Cathedral. Along with Dix, he was one of the contributors to Kirk's collection of essays,* The Apostolic Ministry *(1946).*

28 December 1949

My dear Freddy

This is a belated Christmas letter. I was so rushed that I simply had to leave all my own personal letters till after Christmas. So it brings all my wishes for a more active New Year!

You will have heard that the "Catholicity Group",[1] or what we could collect of it, met some of the "Theological Protestants" at Springfield, St Mary for two and a half days (on the royalties of "Catholicity"!) Michael R., Harry Carp., Austin, Lionel C.R., Gabriel H., Bob Exeter and myself met a group of which Rupp, D. Jenkins, Torrance, Philip Watson, Burleigh (Presby. – a sheer joy, a lovely man) and Nat Micklem[2] were the chief. They are a delightful set of men and I liked them very much. But I really think they have nothing much to teach us. It was very interesting in a way, but we got nowhere. It is all the old sixteenth century stuff warmed up a little and trimmed up a bit – but so extraordinarily jejune and impoverished *in content*. What *can* make them satisfied with it? One rather odd thing Rupp did point out. We make *exactly* the same accusations against each other on a rather different basis. Nobody seemed quite to know what to make of it, but the fact seems indisputable. He made a sort of tabular statement (like "Demant's Tables"). I am very glad we had the meeting. It has quite ascertained me (if that is a possible expression) that we were on the right lines in "Catholicity". I think they were rather shaken to find how very little we had to take account of. I know two of them, at all events, were very chastened.

I had previously been to Aberdeen and preached a University Sermon – they had it all worked out pat – "the first monk in that pulpit for 423 years" etc. There was an overflowing congregation, but no riot! In the evening I preached in the Piskie Cathedral, and to my astonishment most of the Presbie Dons turned up again! They were extraordinarily kind and generous – £16 "travelling expenses" – and gave me a very good but busy time. Donald Mackinnon[3] was

in magnificent form, and is evidently doing a very fine job of work
– immensely respected, though still behaving rather like a Red Indian
at times. But he is *much* more serene and "integrated" than he was at
Oxford. He is certainly finding himself. By the way I lectured also at
Edinburgh and St Andrews, at their request. *And* I met most of the
Presbie delegation who will meet John Derby[4] & Co. on 5 January.
I have refused to go on to that party. It is a sheer waste of time and
money. John will receive the full brunt of the *Institutes* on a "polity
of presbyters" *jure divino* & *de fide*. If he thinks he can get *that* lot
to "take episcopacy into their system", he will have a grand time
explaining.

My Christmas has been rather embittered by receiving 14 pages
from Monsignor Fisher, apparently devoted to proving that there
was widespread "suspicion" and "hostility to almost everything the
bishop try to do". I wrote back agreeing with him and adding further
illustrations, and hinting that perhaps if the bishops tried to do something different it would in time not be so. He countered at once with
another 10 pages elaborating on the suspicion theme and saying it
was all my fault. I sent it to K.O.[5] who told me not to "bicker" with
G.,[6] and suggests I offer to see him. I don't think I shall. It will put
me in quite a false position as the "leader of the opposition" and if
the Bishops make further gaffes I shall be held responsible for any
fuss. I think he is going off it. Anyhow I have sent a stalling answer
and said I have too much to do at present to give it the attention it
deserves. I have got to do a couple of articles for *Time and Tide* and
then my lectures for Sweden as well as some other oddments. I go to
Stockholm on 25th January and the following week to Uppsala and
the one after that to Lund. Then I do a week rather like the "Lambeth
Walk" of Colonial Bishops last year, being rushed round half the
Cathedrals in Sweden to preach on "the Liturgy". I don't know a
word of Swedish except "Sverige Post" on the stamps and that there
is a coin called an "Ore" also from the stamps. Well – now do get
better quickly!

Yours ever affectionately

Gr. Dix, O.S.B.

## Notes

1. The "Catholicity Group" refers to the authors of the report, "Catholicity: A Study of the Conflict of Christian Traditions in the West", presented to the Archbishop of Canterbury, Geoffrey Fisher, in 1947. Those who attended the meeting at Springfield included Dix, Michael Ramsey, Harry Carpenter, Austin Farrer, Lionel Thornton CR, Gabriel Hebert SSM and Robert Mortimer.

2. This group consisted of Gordon Rupp, Daniel Jenkins, Tom Torrance, Philip Watson, John Burleigh and Nathaniel Micklem.

3. Donald MacKinnon was Regius Chair of Moral Philosophy at Aberdeen University from 1947 until he moved to become Norris Hulse Professor of Divinity in the University of Cambridge in 1960. From 1940 to 1947 he had been a tutorial fellow at Keble College, Oxford, where, 20 years earlier, Dix himself had taught.

4. John Rawlinson (1884–1960), Bishop of Derby.

5. Kenneth Kirk (1886–1954), Bishop of Oxford.

6. Geoffrey Fisher (1887–1972), Archbishop of Canterbury.


24 September 1951

My dearest Freddy (in fact my *only* dear Freddy)

I have just turned out your letter of 6th June and realised with a pang that I have done nothing about it! When I arrived I was just scuffling with the surgeons to try to convince them that I really had healed up completely in just half the number of days they said was possible. After x-raying me in bed they admitted it, and ultimately let me out of hospital just a fortnight after the operation. I did twice try to get into Purgatory on the day of the operation (and knew it, very oddly!) but was pulled back by the prayers of my friends. I never was so humbled in my life as by the *hundreds* of letters from people most of whom I had never heard of, saying they were praying for me. Then I had an enchanting week being pulled around Oxford in a bath-chair – the *ideal* way to visit Oxford – to see all my friends and enemies. Then I went down to Cornwall to the moors right on top of Land's End and learned to walk again, three to four miles at a time, and ultimately climbed a five-barred gate – not very fast, but I climbed it eventually. Then I was fetched back for another x-ray, elaborately.camouflaged as "a mere check-up on the stitches" – but they really expected to find a recurrence of the cancer. Of this there is at present no sign, but I have to have x-rays and sigmoidoscope examinations every three months for two years. Since then I have been here and I now manage to get through the whole day (barring the Night Office) from 6.30am to 10.00pm (though I still have to lie

down for a couple of hours in the day – during which it is difficult
not to pray against people!) The *bon Dieu* is really *very* neat in his
ways and *so* reliable.

I was sent to U.S. because the Community there was outgrowing its
buildings and also in debt, with a mortgage on the farm. U.S. building prices are so impossible that I reported to the Abbot that I dared
only attempt a new Chapel and an adaptation of the other buildings, though they really *needed* a monastery as well as Chapel, *and* a
retreat house. So I borrowed $20,000 from a bank, got an architect,
gave out a contract and set forth to raise $35,000 to pay for it – at
the beginning of last October. By the end of October I felt like death
and early in November saw a doctor who sent me to a big New York
surgeon who told me I had got cancer, that the necessary operation
would cost $1,500 at least and put me out of action for eight months.
It was very awkward. If I pulled out then, we couldn't pay the bank
or pay the rest of the contract and St Gregory's would be (literally)
bankrupted. And I could hardly write to the Abbey 3000 miles away
and say "Do you prefer to murder me or bankrupt the Priory?" – it
seemed hardly decent. So, after thinking it out, I decided I had got to
go on and pay for the beastly buildings somehow and then have the
operation. That was what I had been sent under obedience to do, and
I must just trust in God to carry it out. (I was very frightened!) The
really horrid thing was not being able to consult anyone. But if I let
out one squeak to anybody, they were bound to feel a responsibility
to let the Abbot know, and then we should have *both* the bankruptcy
*and* the operation. I think the only person who really suspected anything was Bill Antigua (& Mrs)[1] – but the holiday there *just* made it
possible for me to survive the very heavy "schedule" of speaking etc.
in the spring. They were both *angelic* to me, and the holiday was like
heaven (except for the pain in my belly). Meanwhile I prayed hard for
a new Monastery and the mortgage. Then I went down to Texas and
Louisiana to earn my fare back to England and enough to pay the
Abbot's plane-fare (return) to be at the consecration of the Church.
After that my insides went rather to bits – and at *that* point three
people I didn't know (I don't even know the name of one now, who
acted through a lawyer) and who didn't know each other – sent me
$50,000, $10,000, and $7,000 – the exact amount needed ($60,000)
for the new Monastery (which I had never mentioned to a soul) and
for the mortgage ($7,000) which also nobody knew but myself, the
Prior and the Bursar. (Altogether I raised about $130,000 in that
eleven months. I hit the film-star level of income!) I stayed for the

consecration of the Church in May, flew to New York the next day, and to England the following day, saw the doctor the afternoon I got back, went into hospital and had it all done for free the next week. Doesn't that just show how neatly the Good God can tie up the ends when He chooses? And now, barring a tendency to get tired rather easily and an inability to concentrate for more than three quarters of an hour or so at a time – which they tell me are invariable but passing results of a big operation, I am better than I have been for years – and indeed the surgeons now speak of my realigned alimentary canal in terms of admiration usually reserved for one or two special bits of Venice! And the Community in Michigan move into the new Monastery on 3rd October and the old one will become a retreat house for men – the only one for 500 miles around. The new Church has nine altars and is rather a nice building – and we consecrated it with a great gathering of bishops from all over the Middle West – one for each altar. So *Deo gratias*! Say a "thank you" for me – for I still don't think He has been thanked enough.

On the strength of my operation, I am able to void all outside engagements for a year. This will enable me a) to revise *The Shape of the Liturgy* (having had my own 'shape' revised) – which I find to my surprise is still selling about 1500 copies a year, and is therefore worth keeping up to date, and b) to write a book on the Apostolic Age – which I have begun putting together in scraps and which looks like being rather fun. There are some "accepted positions" which are really only hangovers from the "Liberal generation", which I think can be stood rather neatly on their heads, with definite improvements in the understanding of history, and I propose to try and do it. (No doubt, it will cause fresh screams of rage from certain people – but why not?) The only outside thing I want to keep on is Convocation – anyhow for the present. We have still to have the "show-down" with Geoffrey[2] and Jacky[3] about *Church Relations in England* – though that whole conspiracy shows signs of collapsing ignominiously, with the Non-conformists slapping +Geoffrey's face rather smartly in public next year. Worry about this was one of the reasons for Jacky's thrombosis. I feel desperately sorry for him. He is so very unhappy – and he has sold his soul for an ecclesiastical-political "success" – and has nothing left to give in exchange for it now. I have had some good letters from him since I got back. I think he knew it was all up when the Non-conformists virtually declared that they would do no more with him or +Geoffrey till they had the endorsement of the Lower House of Convocation and he and they all turned and looked at me. (I said nothing at all and looked straight forward). That was the result of my *nem con* motion stymieing "South India" in the Lower House thirteen months ago, just before I went to the U.S. It won't do to be over-confident – but I am pretty sure I can pass a "wrecking amendment" whenever +Geoffrey lets the Lower House have the *Report* – which he is still most unwilling to do. But I had drawn him into pledging his teeth that he *would* do so, by hinting in public that he dare not. He described my conduct as "devilish" at a meeting in Lambeth Palace, and we had a lively correspondence, after which I went off to the U.S. *But* the Non-conformists have steadily refused (actually the Methodists) to carry on the negotiations ever since – until he sends *Church Relations in England* to the Lower House and we know whether he and Jacky can deliver the goods. If there is an October session of Convocation I shall attend it, just in case. But I gather that Mr Attlee's (rather suicidal?) decision may precipitate a dissolution of the Lower House before the session – and perhaps +Geoffrey would prefer to bring it before a new House.

If the Lower House is dissolved with Parliament I shall go off to Scotland at the end of next week (if not, on 15th October) on a sort of "snob's progress" a) to a deer-forest in Inverness, b) to stay in a castle on the Isle of Colonsay, c) for ten days with the Bishop of Argyll and the Isles[4] at Onich, looking right down the Firth of Lorne – the most beautiful spot I know in the world – and some of the best fishing – and do a month "huntin' & shootin' & fishin'" with old friends and really getting the ginger back into me again. (October is usually the best month in the year in the West Highlands). If St Paul was right about "bowels of compassion", I *ought* to be short of them in future!

Meanwhile, it is quite lovely just to be quietly here, with no duties but the choir and the running of the house as Prior, and all the time there is to say one's prayers in. I haven't been in such a blissful state for years. It is a great waste my being alive at all really, because I shall never again be so well prepared (and quite content) to die as I was in May, after expecting it for seven months. But I find that I do quite enjoy being alive, all the same, in this peace. I hope it lasts. Meanwhile we go quietly forward. Kenneth ordained Dom Wulstan Deacon on Sunday. (He comes here for his retreat in November.) Fr Robert (Max)[5] who sends his love, should be making his solemn (life) profession on St Andrew's day and we have five postulants (three priests, two lay) coming in the next three weeks. Fr Abbot is away, staying at the Abbey of Pierre-qui-vire in Yonne, France, and com-

ing back via le Bec and Mont-César Abbeys at the end of next week
– so I am in charge until then, but it is very unexacting. (The brethren are good – all except one, whom I beat up this morning. He is
now good.) I am correcting the proofs of a set of essays by Lutheran
professors from Uppsala for Dacre Press. The fruits of my trip to
Uppsala and Lund in the Spring of 1950. Very good, very anti-liberal
– and one Riesenfeld comes out with a vigorous pro-*Shaliach* blast
which will upset the Protestants in this country nicely. Give my love
to Humphrey and Marjorie.[6] Has Humphrey been ordained yet? Let
me have *de vos nouvelles*.

Ever yours affectionately

Gregory O.S.B.

**Notes**

1. Nathaniel William Davis (1903–66) was Bishop of Antigua during 1944–
52. He was in the year below Dix at Merton, matriculating in 1921.
2. Geoffrey Fisher, Archbishop of Canterbury.
3. John Rawlinson, Bishop of Derby.
4. Thomas Hannay (1887–1970), Bishop of Argyll and the Isles.
5. Maxwell Charles Petitpierre was also an undergraduate at Merton,
matriculating in 1921. He joined the Community at Nashdom in 1948, taking
the name Robert.
6. Marjorie and Humphrey are Frederick Green's wife and son. Humphrey
Green was ordained deacon on 20 December 1951 and joined the Community
of the Resurrection in 1962, taking the name Benedict.

# Bibliography

This bibliography lists, in chronological order, all of Dix's books and pamphlets, including those published posthumously, together with those articles and chapters cited in this volume. A full bibliography, including book reviews, can be found in Simon Bailey's biography, *A Tactful God*, Gracewing, 1995.

'The Revealing Church', *Laudate* 8 (1930), pp. 24–46.

'The Christian Passover', *Laudate* 13 (1935), pp. 2–18; also published as *Mass of the Pre-Sanctified*, CLA, 1935.

*The Apostolic Tradition of St Hippolytus*, SPCK, 1937; 2nd edn (ed. Henry Chadwick), SPCK, 1968.

'The Idea of "the Church" in the Primitive Liturgies', in G. Hebert (ed.), *The Parish Communion*, SPCK, 1937; also published as a pamphlet by SPCK.

'Consecration', in K. Mackenzie (ed.), *The Liturgy*, SPCK, 1938.

*A Detection of Aumbries*, Dacre Press, 1942.

*The Question of Anglican Orders: Letters to a Layman*, Dacre Press, 1944.

*The Shape of the Liturgy*, Dacre Press, 1945; a new edition, with an introduction by Simon Jones, was published by Continuum in 2005.

*Theology of Confirmation in Relation to Baptism*, Dacre Press, 1946.

'Ministry in the Early Church', in K. Kirk (ed.), *Apostolic Ministry*, Hodder & Stoughton, 1946, pp. 183–303.

*Dixit Cranmer et non Timuit*, Dacre Press, 1948; originally published as two articles in the *Church Quarterly Review*.

*The Power and Wisdom of God*, Dacre Press, 1948.

'Catholicism Today', *Time and Tide*, 4 February 1950, 107–8; 11 February 1950, 131–2.

*Jew and Greek*, Dacre Press, 1953.

*The Image and Likeness of God*, Dacre Press, 1953.

*God's Way with Man*, Dacre Press, 1954.

*Jurisdiction in the Early Church*, CLA, 1975; originally published as a series of articles in *Laudate* in 1937 and 1938.

*Holy Order*, CLA, 1976.

# Acknowledgements

The Author and Publisher are grateful for permission to reproduce material under copyright from the following copyright holders. Every effort has been made to trace copyright ownership, and apology is made to those unacknowledged or not traced. The Author and Publisher would be grateful to be informed of any omissions, and full acknowledgement will be made in future editions.

Material from *Jurisdiction in the Early Church* (1975), and also from *Holy Order* (1976), both works by Gregory Dix, are reproduced by permission of the Church Literature Association (The Church Union).

Material from *The Parish Communion* (1937), edited by Gabriel Hebert, and *The Liturgy* (1938), edited by Kenneth Mackenzie, are reproduced by permission of SPCK.

Material from *The Shape of the Liturgy* (new edition, 2005), by Gregory Dix, is reproduced by permission of Continuum International Publishing Group.

# Index of Names

# Index of Subjects